First Edition 1997
Reprinted 1999
Reprinted 2001

Conversation in Action

• Let´s Talk

by Edward R. Rosset

Editorial Stanley

Escrito por / Written by
Edward R. Rosset
Miembro del Colegio de Licenciados de Filosofía y Letras de Euskadi.
Member of the Bachelor of Arts Association of Euskadi.

Editado por / Edited by
Editorial Stanley

Diseño y Maquetación / Lay out
Angela Gómez Martín

Diseño portada / Front Page design
Esquema

Ilustrado por / Illustrated by
Daniel Redondo

Imprime / Printers
Imprenta Berekintza

© Editorial Stanley
Apdo. 207 - 20300 IRUN - SPAIN
Telf. 943 64 04 12 - Fax. 943 64 38 63
www.libross.com

I.S.B.N. 84-7873-326-4
Dep. Leg. BI-1325-01

Primera Edición / First Edition 1997
Reimpresión / Reprinted 1999
Reimpresión / Reprinted 2001

Introducción:

Conversation in action es un libro diseñado para profesores. Las 50 unidades de que consta el libro son el resultado de muchos años de experiencia en el área de los idiomas. Recoge la problemática de muchísimos profesores que tienen dificultades a la hora de hacer que los alumnos hablen en inglés. Otros tienen dificultad en encontrar temas de qué hablar, sin estarse repitiendo continuamente.

Por una causa o por otra, la experiencia demuestra que los profesores se pasan la hora entera hablando mientras que los alumnos responden con monosílabos. Este libro proporcionan al profesor infinidad de preguntas sobre un tema determinado además de ideas interactivas; con ello se crea una atmósfera apropiada para que los alumnos se expresen en inglés.

El libro consta de 50 unidades. En cada unidad se desarrolla un tema diferente. Contiene 40 preguntas sobre cada tópico. Completan la unidad un dibujo y un texto sobre lo que hay que hacer preguntas, y respuestas así como dar explicaciones; también se forman parejas o grupos para discutir, comentar sobre aseveraciones y para decir si algo es correcto o no.

Introduction:

Conversation in action is a book designed for teachers. The 50 units that make up the book are the result of many years of experience in the area of languages. It tries to solve the problems of many teachers that have difficulties in making pupils speak in English. Others have a hard time in finding topics to speak about, without repeating themselves day after day .

For one reason or other, the experience shows that teachers spend the whole class speaking, while pupils answer with monosyllables. This book provides the teacher with endless questions, besides interactive ideas; with this, an appropriate atmosphere is created for the students to express themselves in English.

The book is made up of 50 units; a different topic being worked out in each unit. There are 40 questions about each topic. An illustration and a text about which the pupils have to make questions and answers as well as give explanations, complete the unit. Couples or groups are made up to discuss, to comment about assertions and to decide whether some things are true or false.

· Index

1 · Family 2
2 · Games and sports 4
3 · Married life or Living together 6
4 · Holidays / Vacations 8
5 · Shopping 10
6 · At school 12
7 · Films 14
8 · Housekeeping 16
9 · Jobs 18
10 · Military Service 20
11 · Television 22
12 · Christmas 24
13 · Driving 26
14 · Travelling 28
15 · Learning a foreign language 30
16 · In a restaurant 32
17 · Success in life 34
18 · Hotels 36
19 · At the bank 38
20 · Pubs 40
21 · At the Doctor's 42
22 · At the hospital 44
23 · Natural Medicine 46
24 · Occultism 48
25 · Hypnotism-Telepathy 50
26 · Collecting things 52
27 · At the dentist 54
28 · At the hairdresser's 56
29 · At the zoo 58

30	· At the beach	60
31	· Tourism	62
32	· Being a king	64
33	· Politics	66
34	· Religions	68
35	· Popular festivals	70
36	· Party time	72
37	· A department store	74
38	· Studying or working	76
39	· Having a baby	78
40	· Cruising	80
41	· A desert Island	82
42	· Reading	84
43	· Professions	86
44	· Actors	88
45	· Football	90
46	· Policemen	92
47	· A street market	94
48	· Writing	96
49	· Painting	98
50	· Sailing	100

Conversation in Action
- Let´s Talk

1 · Family

Glossary
married
age
advantage
disadvantage
wives
husbands
allowed
disabled
share
nowadays
teach
quarrel
reasons
make up
apologize
believe
presents

Description of the scene:

Suggested roleplays and dialogues

· In pairs, make up short dialogues. You and your sister are laying the table.
· In pairs, make up a dialogue in which your sister is doing the cooking.
· In groups of three, think up a conversation in which you three are clearing the table after dinner.

Make comments on the following statements

· It's nice to live in a quiet place away from the traffic, in the suburbs.
· It's nice to have many children.
· The husband and the wife should both go to work.
· The children should make their own beds.
· Children should go to a nursery.

Questions on the scene

· How many people are there in the picture?
· What are they doing?
· What has the older girl in her hands?
· What has the father got in his hand?
· What about the boy?
· What's the mother doing?
· What's over the table?
· What's the father wearing?
· And the rest of the family?
· What's on the table?

True or false. Give reasons

· Arabs are allowed to have four wives.
· Arab women are allowed to have four husbands.
· Nowadays families have an average of six children.
· Many wives go to work nowadays.
· In the old days men didn't do the housework.
· Nowadays married people have to choose between having children or having a car.

Questions based on language functions

· What does the father say to the children if he wants them to lay the table?
· What do the children say if they are watching an interesting programme on TV?
· What does the father say if he wants them to switch off the TV?
· How does the husband say to the wife that he would like to have a coffee after dinner?

Robert and Lucy are married. They've been happily married for fifteen years. Robert works in a factory, he's a machine operator. He works from 8 to 3. Lucy works at the local supermarket. She's the supervisor of the check-out. She works part time, from 10 to 2. They have four children, Mark, 14, John, 13, Hilda, 11 and Jane, 8. Mark and John go to St. Mary's Secondary school of the local County council. Hilda and Jane are still at Primary School. They live in a little cottage in Park Lane. The back of the house gives on to the park and it's a very quiet place. There is no noise, no traffic. The only noise they hear comes from the children playing in the park, or the birds in the trees. The two boys often go out with their friends at the weekends. Sometimes they go to the school sports grounds to play football. The girls like to stay at home watching TV or playing in the garden. They have a little Yorkshire Terrier. They all like playing with the dog.

Questions

1. How long have Robert and Lucy been married?
2. Where does Robert work?
3. What are his working hours?
4. What does Lucy do?
5. Does she work full time?
6. What are the ages of the four children?
7. Which school do the boys go to?
8. What about the girls?
9. Where do they live?
10. What's at the back of the house?
11. Is it a noisy street?
12. What's the only noise they can hear?
13. What do the boys do at the weekends?
14. What about the girls?
15. What sort of dog do they have?

Family

1. What's your first name?
2. What's your surname (family name)?
3. What's your mother's name?
4. Do you have any brothers or sisters?
5. What are their names?
6. What's your father's name?
7. Do you have a grandfather or grandmother?
8. How old are they?
9. Do you have any uncles or aunts?
10. How many cousins have you got?
11. What are their names?
12. Are they older than you?
13. How old are they?
14. Are they boys or girls?
15. Where do your cousins live?
16. Where do your grandparents live?
17. What does your father do?
18. Where does your mother work?
19. Does your father have a car?
20. What kind of car is it?
21. Do you know the make?
22. What does your brother do?
23. What about your sisters? What do they do?
24. Do you live in a house or in a flat?
25. Do you have your own room?
26. Does your brother or sister have his/her own room?
27. What do you have in your room?
28. Can you describe your house or flat?
29. Do you have a garden or a balcony?
30. Have you got a pet?
31. What kind of pet have you got?
32. What's its name?
33. How old is it?
34. Does your mother let you have a pet in the house?
35. How do you get on with your brother/sister?
36. Do you quarrel or argue with him/her?
37. Do you go to the same school as your brother/sister?
38. Do your grandparents live with you?
39. Do you have a great-grandfather/grandmother?
40. Do your grandparents give you any pocket money?

2 · Games and sports

Glossary
game
hardest
dangerous
laziest
harm
championship
team
referee
mistakes
match
score
chess
to draw/tie
to climb
to keep fit

Description of the scene:

Suggested roleplays and dialogues

· In pairs, make up short dialogues in which one of pupils explains to the other the difference between sports and games.
· In groups of three, make up short conversations in which the pupils comment on the difference between sport to keep fit and sport for competition.
· In pairs, the students can speak about their favourite sports.
· In pairs, ask them to make a list of all the sports they can remember. See which pair remembers most.

Make comments on the following statements:

· Competition is better than sports for keeping fit.
· Individual sport is better than team sports.
· People should go in for sport every day not just at weekends.
· Running a marathon is good for health.
· Running is good for women.
· Competing is good for health.

Questions on the scene

· What's the woman in the first picture doing?
· What's the woman on the top right picture doing?
· What's the man on the bottom left picture doing?
· What's the man on the bottom right picture doing?
· What are they all wearing?

True or false. Give reasons

· In sport, teams compete one against the other.
· Football and basketball are games.
· If both sides score the same number of goals it is a draw.
· At weekends many people go in for games.
· Amateurs are very well paid.

Questions based on language functions

· What does the referee say to the players when the match is going to start?
· What does the starter say to the ahtletes when the race is about to start and when they must get to their marks?
· How does the captain of a football team say to one of the players that he has to replace the injured goal keeper?
· How do you think the finish line judge will tell an athlete that he still has another lap to go?

'Mr Jones, what's the difference between games and sports?' 'Well, Jimmy,' said the teacher smiling at the little boy sitting at the front, 'a game is usually a competition between two teams or two people. The side that scores more points wins. We speak about playing a game of football, of tennis, cricket, baseball, basketball, rugby, volley-ball, hockey, ping-pong, chess and many others. In a game, a person or a team wins and the other side loses. Of course, they can also draw or tie; sometimes it's called equalize; another expression for a draw is two all, three all, or two to two, three to three, etc.'

Sport, on the other hand, is more individual. You don't usually score points. You don't 'play' or 'practise' a sport. You 'go in for' or 'take up' sport. Running, jumping, throwing, swimming, walking, climbing, cycling, doing gymnastics, etc, are all sports. Many people go in for sports or play games at the weekends just to keep fit.'

Questions

1. Where's this conversation taking place?
2. What's the name of the teacher?
3. What's the name of the little boy?
4. What does the boy want to know?
5. Where's he sitting?
6. What does the teacher do when he answers the question?
7. What is a game?
8. Which side wins in a game?
9. Give the names of two games not mentioned in the reading.
10. Do the same with sports.
11. When the two teams have the same number of points, they.
12. You play games, but what about sport? You.
13. Why do some people play games at weekends?
14. Do you score points in sport?
15. What's usually more individual, a game or a sport?

Games & sports

1. What's your favourite sport?
2. What games do you usually play?
3. Mention all the games and sports you can think of.
4. What's the so called 'sport king'?
5. What sport do people practise, or go in for, in your country?
6. Mention the games that the English play.
7. «   «   «   « Americans play.
8. Do you do any sport?
9. Are you good at any games or sports?
10. Which do you think is the hardest sport?
11. Which do you think is the most dangerous?
12. Which do you think is the laziest?
13. Do you think sport is good for the health?
14. Can you mention some benefits sport provides?
15. Is there any harm that sport may do to you?
16. What do you think of running?
17. What are the advantages of running?
18. What are the disadvantages?
19. What do you think of running marathons?
20. What do you think of competing in thriathlons?
21. What is the difference between professional and amateur sport?
22. What do you think of professional sport?
23. Do you think professional sport should be paid?
24. Do you know any names of professional sportsmen?
25. Mention some names of professional players or sportsmen.
26. What about sports women? do you know any?
27. Do you know how many hours professionals train?
28. Would you like to be a professional sporstman/woman?
29. Would you like to go to the Olympic Games?
30. Do you watch them on TV?
31. Which sports do you like to watch most?
32. What do you think of football on TV?
33. Do you like watching the World Cup?
34. Do you know which team won the last championship?
35. Where did the championship take place?
36. Have any Olympic Games taken place in your country?
37. Would you like to help in the stadium?
38. What would you like to do?
39. Have you ever been a referee? what do you think of them?
40. Do referees make mistakes? Should a match be repeated?

3 · Married life or Living together

Glossary
surname
aunt
uncle
cousin
kind
the make
quarrel
argue
death
percent
hell
arguing
tiredness
tend

Description of the scene:

Suggested roleplays and dialogues

- In pairs, make up a conversation between a grandfather and his grandson.
- In pairs, make up a conversation about cars.
- In groups of three, make up a conversation about houses. Where they should be located, etc.
- In groups of four, make up a conversation about pets at home.

Make comments on the following statements.

- In the old days people didn't get divorced.
- Discussions start when people are tired.
- Arguing in front of the children.
- Living in a house or in a flat.
- Having a pet in the house.
- Living with grandparents.

Questions on the scene

- What's the man doing in the first picture?
- How old do you think he is?
- Where's the car in the second picture?
- Is it an expensive car?
- Is that a flat in the third picture?
- Are there any trees?
- What's there in the fourth picture?
- What has he got with him?
- What's he carrying?

True or false. Give reasons

- You can have a garden in a flat.
- Brothers and sisters argue very often.
- Grandparents often take the children for a walk.
- Children often live with their cousins in the same house.

Questions based on language functions

- What does the boy say to his sister if he wants to watch another programme?
- What does the girl say if she doesn't want to change the channel?
- What does the child say to the grandfather if he wants to go to the park?
- How does the grandfather say to the child that they can't go out because it's raining?

Not many years ago, when two people got married it was for good, 'until death separated them'. Very few marriages ended up in divorce. Nowadays, about fifty percent of the couples that get married separate after a few years of living together. Married life can be very pleasant if there is love between husband and wife, or it can be hell if they keep arguing and criticising each other all the time. Psycologists say that couples should watch for tiredness. When people are tired after a long day at the office, they tend to be irritable and answer back. Experts say that we must be thankful for what we have, and repeat to ourselves that we are very happy. If a person repeats it many times a day he/she will end up believing it, and then, he/she will really be happy.

Questions

1. Was divorce common a few years ago?
2. For how long were people married?
3. How many couples get divorced nowadays?
4. When can married life be pleasant?
5. When can married life be hell?
6. What do psycologists say?
7. What happens after a long day at the office?
8. What do experts say?
9. What happens when you repeat something many times to yourself?
10. What will happen if you believe that you are happy?

Married life or Living together

1. Are you married? if not, would you like to get married?
2. What is the best age to get married?
3. How old were your parents when they got married?
4. How many children would you like to have?
5. What are the advantges and disadvantages of having one or two children?
6. What are the advantages and disadvantages of having many?
7. What are the advantages and disadvantages of married life?
8. Would you live with your boy/girlfriend without being married?
9. What are the advantages of this living together arrangement?
10. What are the disadvantages of it?
11. Do you believe in equality between husband and wife?
12. What do you think about Arabs' wives?
13. What happens if they don't obey their husbands?
14. What happens to adulterous women in an Islam country?
15. What happens to aduterous men in an Islam country?
16. How many wives are Arabs allowed to have?
17. How many husbands are Arabs allowed to have?
18. How many concubines can an Arab have?
19. What other societies or religions allow several wives?
20. What other societies or religions allow several husbands?
21. What is the most important aspect in married life?
22. Is sex the only attraction?
23. Would you get married to a disabled person?
24. Do you think men should share the housework?
25. Should women go to work?
26. Can a woman with six children go to work?
27. What's more important, work or children?
28. Why don't people have more children nowadays?
29. Will you teach your children to make the beds, etc.?
30. Why do you think married couples quarrel?
31. What are the main reasons for quarrelling?
32. Who is usually right, the husband or the wife?
33. Do you quarrel very often with your boy/girlfriend?
34. Who makes up usually?
35. Do you ever apologize to him/her?
36. What do you do when you make up?
37. Do you believe in presents?
38. Should a husband give his wife a present occasionally?
39. What about vice versa?
40. Can couples that quarrel often, be happy?

4. Holidays / Vacations

Glossary
spend
younger
to be over
cruising
abroad
waiter/
waitress
to book
to be like
trek
trail

Description of the scene:

Suggested roleplays and dialogues

- In pairs, act out a roleplay between two persons who have been to an organized holiday/vacation.
- In pairs, act out a roleplay between two people who like to go on their own.
- In pairs, act out a roleplay between two people who like to go on a trek.

Make comments on the following statements:

- A camping holiday.
- A cruising holiday.
- Spending your holiday by the sea.
- Spending your holiday in the mountains.
- Reading during the holidays.

Questions on the scene

- What's the girl in the first picture doing?
- What's the girl in the second picture doing?
- Where's she?
- What are the two people in the third picture doing?
- What's the man in the fourth picture doing?

True or false. Give reasons

- More people prefer summer holidays than winter holidays.
- People from the north of Europe like to spend their holidays in the sun.
- Many students spend their holidays learning another language.
- Medieval banquets are terribly expensive.

Questions based on language functions

- How does the husband ask the wife if she wants to go camping?
- How does the wife tell her husband that she prefers to stay at good hotels?
- What does the husband say to inform his wife that they haven't got enough money for good hotels?
- How does the wife say that she prefers to stay at home?

Some people like to have their holidays/vacations organized. They book it a year in advance so they know which hotel they're staying at, how much it's going to cost, what the beach is like, what the food is like, and what souvenirs they are going to buy.

Others like to go into the unknown world without any foresight. They take the car and stop wherever they like. They sleep in their own caravan or in a cheap hotel. These are the adventurous types, usually with a couple of children. They are always looking for a nice deserted beach all for themselves. There is the third type - people who are much more intrepid. These are the ones that sail around the world in a small yacht; trek across the Pyrenees; cross over the Alps following Hannibal's trail; or do an 8,000m. climb in the Himalayas.

Questions

1. What do some people like?
2. How long in advance do they book the hotel?
3. Do they know how much the hotel is going to cost?
4. Do they know what the food is like?
5. Do these people know what souvenirs they are going to buy?
6. Some other people take their own car, where do they stop?
7. Where do they sleep?
8. Do these people have any children?
9. What are they always looking for?
10. About the third type of people; give two more examples of things they are likely to do.

Holidays / Vacations

1. Where do you usually spend your holidays?
2. Do you go with your family?
3. Where did you go when you were younger?
4. Do you prefer to swim in the sea or in a swimming-pool?
5. What do you think of places like Benidorm?
6. What do you think of spending a holiday in your grandfather's village?
7. Are there people of your age there?
8. What do you do in the mornings?
9. What about the afternoons?
10. What do you do in the evenings?
11. Do you spend a lot of money during your holidays?
12. How much pocket money do you get on holidays?
13. Do you spend more than at home?
14. How do you feel when your holidays are over?
15. Would you like to spend your holidays cruising in the Mediterranean?
16. Which do you prefer winter or summer holidays?
17. What do you think about taking all your holidays at the same time?
18. Do you think it's better to take holidays in parts?
19. What is better to spend holidays with the family or with friends?
20. Have you ever been camping? if so, where?
21. What do you think of camping?
22. What are the advantages and disadvantages of camping?
23. Have you ever been to a medieval banquet?
24. What are they like?
25. If you could, what sort of holiday would you like to have?
26. Do you take any school books to revise?
27. What about reading? do you read during your holidays?
28. Do you meet any English-speaking people during your holidays?
29. Do you practise any other languages?
30. What do you think of spending your holidays learning languages?
31. What do you think of working camps abroad?
32. Have you ever been to one? what are the benefits or advantages?
33. What are the disadvantages of working camps?
34. Have you ever considered spending your holidays helping people in the third world?
35. What do you think of working during your holidays?
36. Would you like to work as a waiter or waitress?
37. What do you think of people who work in summer?
38. Have yor ever had to stay at home because you had examinations in September?
39. Are holidays short or long? How long should they be?
40. Should holidays be a time for reading?

5. Shopping

Glossary
grocer's
yourself
mail
antique
auction
spendthrift
to put on
bother
in a hurry
enjoy
to fill
huge
brim
tills

Description of the scene:

Suggested roleplays and dialogues

- In pairs, act out a roleplay between the shop keeper and the client in an old shop.
- In pairs, act out a roleplay between a client and the girl at the till in the local supermarket.
- In groups, make up conversations in favour and against the old grocer's shops and modern supermarkets.

Make comments on the following statements:

- Hypermarkets are expensive and too far from the town centres.
- In the old grocer's shop the grocer was a friend of everybody.
- Women enjoy buying things, men don't.
- Buying things by mail is better.
- People steal things in a supermarket.

Questions on the scene

- How many people can you see in the picture?
- What's the woman doing?
- What has she got in her hand?
- What's she holding with her left hand?
- Has she done a lot of shopping?
- What does the man at the far end do?

True or false. Give reasons

- In a supermarket you have many things to choose from.
- The attention you get is very impersonal.
- In large supermarkets there are many special offers.
- Men enjoy shopping.
- The Queen of England often goes to the supermarket.

Questions based on language functions

- How does a customer ask an attendant in a supermarket where the tins of asparagus are?
- What does the attendant say to direct him/her?
- What will a customer say to the cashier in a supermarket if they'll accept his/her credit card?
- How will the cashier say that they don't accept that credit card?

I remember going shopping with my grandmother. She didn't bother to put her shoes on. She went in her old slippers. The local grocer's was at the corner of the street. There, she would meet three or four women and have a nice chat while waiting for the grocer to serve them. They were never in a hurry and enjoyed the waiting time. Old Mr Robinson wrote on a piece of paper, in pencil, every item they bought, and then added up the quantities using only his head... and sometimes his fingers. Kind, Mrs. Robinson used to give me a sweet or a candy for helping my grandmother to carry the shopping bag.

Nowadays, the young married couple jump into their small family car on a Saturday afternoon and drive to the Hypermarket, outside town. They fill a huge trolley to the brim and join a long queue at one of the 25 tills. They pay with their credit card and push the trolley to the car. Then, they drive back home, park as near their place as possible, and carry home twenty plastic bags each.

Questions

1. What does the writer remember?
2. Did his grandmother put her shoes on?
3. What did she wear when going shopping?
4. Where was the local grocer's?
5. What did the women do while waiting to be served?
6. How did Mr Robinson find out the total sum?
7. Did he use an adding machine?
8. What did Mr Robinson's wife give the writer?
9. Why did she give it to him?
10. Where do people do their shopping nowadays?
11. How do they go there?
12. How do they carry their shopping?
13. How many tills are there?
14. Do they pay cash?
15. How many plastic bags have they got?

Shopping

1. Do you ever go shopping?
2. What do you think of the small grocer's at the corner?
3. What's a department store?
4. What's a hypermarket?
5. What's a supermarket?
6. Where are the hypermarkets placed?
7. What's the difference between them?
8. What do you think of shopping on a Saturday afternoon in the hypermarket?
9. What are the advantages and disadvantages of them?
10. Do you save money in the large supermarkets?
11. Do you enjoy buying clothes or things for yourself?
12. Do you like buying presents for other people?
13. What do you think of shopping by mail?
14. Do you receive any catalogues regularly?
15. What are the advantages of this kind of shopping?
16. What are the disadvantages?
17. What do you think of street markets?
18. Do you visit them on Saturday or Sunday morning?
19. Do you think it is cheaper to buy there?
20. What sort of things are cheaper there?
21. What about the quality in the street markets?
22. Have you visited a street antique market?
23. Is there a famous one in your country?
24. Have you heard about «Petticoat Lane» in London?
25. Have you ever been to an auction?
26. What do you think of that system of buying things?
27. What are the advantages of an auction?
28. What are the disadvantages?
29. What do you think of men doing the shopping?
30. Do you look at the prices when you go shopping?
31. Are you a spendthrift?
32. What's the difference between men and women when shopping?
33. Are men careful with money?
34. What things do men like to buy?
35. What things do women enjoy buying?
36. What is the best day of the week for shopping?
37. At what time do you usually go to the supermarket?
38. Have you ever checked a supermarket bill? why?/ why not?
39. How do you think the Queen of England does her shopping?
40. What sort of things does she buy?

6 · At school

Glossary
most
least
there
should be
male
subject
worst
to be born
lucky
wrecked
desks
inherited
torn out
scribbled
hungry

Description of the scene:

Suggested roleplays and dialogues

· In pairs, act out a conversation between the teacher and a bad student.
· In pairs, act out a conversation in favour and against modern schools.
· In groups of three, speak about the advantages and disadvantages of staying at school for lunch.

Make comments on the following statements:

· Modern schools are more efficient than the old ones.
· The number of pupils in the classes is smaller.
· Women teachers are better than men teachers.
· Nowadays most schools have dining-rooms.

Questions on the scene

· What's the girl carrying in her hand and in the bag? Where's she going?
· What's the woman doing in the classroom?
· What do you think the teacher is telling the young student?
· What's the girl doing in her desk?
· What are they all wearing?

True or false. Give reasons

· There is no corporal punishment in schools nowadays.
· Most children have lunch at school.
· Teaching methods are the same as fifty years ago.
· Anybody can be a teacher.
· Students must be at school until they are sixteen.

Questions based on language functions

· How do students greet the teacher?
· What does the teacher tell the students to do first thing in the morning?
· How does a pupil ask the teacher if he/she doesn't understand his/her explanations?
· What do the pupils say to the teacher at the end of the day?

In 1912, when my grandfather was born, very few people were lucky enough to go to school. My grandpa had to walk four miles to go to the wrecked building that served as a school. In the same classroom, about twenty boys and girls of different ages sat at hundred-year-old desks. Their books had been inherited from more advanced pupils and many of their pages had been torn out or had been badly scribbled on. The maps on the wall had seen better times and the frontiers of many of the countries shown had already changed.

Almost a hundred years afterwards, school children are collected by a school bus and are taken to a large modern building with a huge playground. Their classrooms are large and well lit. Young trained teachers take about a dozen pupils at a time. They use modern teaching methods and have laboratories at their disposal. Half a dozen cooks prepare a well balanced lunch for five hundred hungry youngsters. At five o'clock the school buses deposit them carefully outside their homes.

Questions

1. When was the writer's grandfather born?
2. Did many people go to school in those days?
3. How far did his grandfather walk to go to school?
4. What was the building like?
5. How many children were in the same classroom?
6. Were they all of the same age?
7. Can you describe the books they used?
8. Were the maps on the wall new?
9. How do school children go to school nowadays?
10. What are the classrooms like?
11. What sort of teachers do they have nowadays?
12. Do they still use old methods?
13. How many cooks work in the kitchen?
14. How many children go to those schools?
15. At what time do they go back home?

At school

1. Are you studying or working?
2. What are your teachers like?
3. Describe the teacher you like most
4. Describe the teacher you like least
5. What are the qualities a teacher should have?
6. What are the faults a teacher shouldn't have?
7. How many students are there in your class?
8. How many students do you think there should be in a class?
9. What do you prefer a male teacher or a female teacher?
10. What do you do if you don't understand the teacher's explanation?
11. Do the pupils usually understand the teacher's explanation?
12. What is the most common punishment in your school?
13. What do you think of corporal pusnishment?
14. Can you describe some of these punishments?
15. Compare the schools 50 years ago and a modern school.
16. Are the teaching methods the same?
17. What are the advantages of modern methods?
18. What are the disadvantages of modern methods?
19. What are your memories of your younger school days?
20. Do you remember the first day you went to school?
21. How did you learn to multiply?
22. How did you learn to read and write?
23. Do you remember the first book you ever read?
24. Do you remember your first teacher? what was he/she like?
25. What was your classroom like?
26. Do you think little children are happy at school?
27. At what age do you think boys and girls should leave school?
28. At what age do they leave school?
29. At what age will/did you leave school?
30. What subjet do you like best?
31. What subject do you like least?
32. Do you study languages at school? Which languages?
33. At what age did you start to learn English?
34. Did you start at school or in a private class?
35. Did you have lunch at school?
36. Can you describe the food you had?
37. How long did you stop for lunch?
38. Did you like the first lesson in the afternoon?
39. Which is the worst time for studing?
40. Have you ever gone to sleep during a lesson?

7 · Films

Glossary
screen
dubbed
used to be
stuntman
growth
perishable
to crowd
eager
to risk
goers
blood

Description of the scene:

Suggested roleplays and dialogues

· In pairs, act out the conversation between the two men in picture two.
· In pairs, act out a conversation between the film director and a film star.
· In pairs, act out a telephone conversation between two lovers.

Make comments on the following statements

· Violence films are good/bad for children.
· Terror films make children afraid.
· Love scenes should be considered normal.
· It's better watch a film on the little/big screen.
· Film stars shouldn't get so much money.

Questions on the scenes

· What sort of film is the first picture?
· What about the second picture?
· And the third?
· What do you think the woman on the fourth picture does?
· What are the men doing in the second picture?

True or false. Give reasons

· Films haven't changed in the last fifty years.
· There are more cinemas now than fifty years ago.
· The life of a film star is very hard.
· Films in black and white were more interesting.
· European films are more popular than American films.

Questions based on language functions

· What does the film director say to an actress if he wants to invite her to dinner?
· What does the actress say to refuse the invitation?
· What does the film director say to the extras in a film in which they have to repeat the 'battle'?
· How does the main actress say to the director that she is tired and wants a rest?

When the brothers Louis and Auguste Lumière showed in Paris the first two films ever produced *Workers leaving the factory Lumière* and *The arrival of the train*, in 1895, they didn't even dream of the incredible growth of the film industry a century later. Unfortunately the first films were made of perishable material (celluloid). and nothing is left of them. Over thirty years had to pass before any significant advance was made in the making of films. Nowadays we think it's incredible that people would crowd in little rooms eager to watch the silent films of the 1920's. The heroes of those films often risked their lives to shoot really dangerous scenes on the roofs of high buildings. They would save their fainting heroines at the last minute from an oncoming train or a falling building.

Today no film director would risk the precious life of a highly paid film star in one of those scenes. Well trained stunt men do most of them.

The taste of cinema goers has also changed quite a lot. People, nowadays, like to see true to life action; killings, massacres, blood splashed all over the place. The more enemies the hero kills the better.

Questions

1. Who invented the cinematograph?
2. What were the names of the first two films ever produced?
3. Did the Lumière brothers think the film industry would grow so much?
4. What sort of material was used to make the old films?
5. How many years had to pass before any advance was made in the making of films?
6. Did the actors and actresses speak in the early times?
7. Did the heroes of the films in those days risk their lives?
8. Why were the scenes dangerous?
9. Give another situation in which the heroine is saved at the last minute by the hero.
10. Would a film director risk the life of a film star nowadays?
11. Why not?
12. Which people do the dangerous scenes?
13. Has the taste of cinema goers changed?
14. What do people like to see nowadays?
15. Do they like to see blood?

Films

1. What sort of films do you like?
2. Do you like films in black and white?
3. What do you think of old films?
4. What do you think of modern films?
5. Was there a lot of sex in films before?
6. What about modern films, is there a lot of sex?
7. Do many people go to the cinema nowadays?
8. Are there many cinemas in your home town?
9. Are the cinemas big or small?
10. Do you think modern films are good or bad?
11. What's the difference between old and modern films?
12. What do you think of violence in films?
13. Do you like horror films?
14. Can you sleep well after seeing a horror film?
15. What's the best film you have ever seen?
16. Why do you like it so much?
17. What's the most expensive film ever made?
18. Do you like watching films on TV?
19. What's the difference between a big screen and a little one?
20. What are the advantages of watching the film on TV?
21. Have you ever seen a film in the original version?
22. Do you think films should be dubbed?
23. Do you like films with subtitles?
24. What do you think of American films?
25. Do you find any difference between American films and British films?
26. Do you like Spanish films? What do you think of them?
27. What about French films?
28. What about Italian films?
29. What do you think about the European film industry?
30. Do you think films should have a state subsidy?
31. Which is most important in a film, the story? the acting?
32. Which film star do you like best? Why?
33. Are film stars better actors and actresses than they used to be?
34. What do you think of the acting in your country?
35. Which films in your country have won Oscars?
36. Would you like to lead the life of a film star?
37. What are the disadvantages of being famous?
38. Would you do a love scene?
39. Do film stars do the dangerous scenes?
40. Would you like to be a stuntman? Why?

8 · Housekeeping

Glossary
to share
the washing
hoovers
dishwasher
worth
appliances
ironing
fireplace
to sew
deep freezer
fridge
chores
dusting
get used to

Description of the scene:

Suggested roleplays and dialogues

- In pairs, act out the conversation between the mother and a daughter. The mother wants the girl to make her bed, dust the furniture, etc.
- In pairs, act out a conversation between husband and wife when one of them goes out to work.
- In pairs, act out a conversation between wife and husband about the distribution of jobs.

Make comments on the following statements

- Husbands should stay in bed all morning.
- The kitchen is the women's place.
- Men earn enough to keep a family.
- Women should look after the babies.

Questions on the scene

- What's the man wearing on his head?
- What's he doing?
- What time of the day is it?
- Did he do the washing up the night before?
- How would you describe his expression?

True or false. Give reasons

- Housewives get a good salary.
- Modern appliances make life easier.
- Our grandmothers scrubbed the floors on their knees.
- A dishwasher is not very useful.
- In the old days people cooked in a brass pot hanging over the fire.

Questions based on language functions

- How does the repairman say to the housewife that the washing machine is broken and that she'll have to do the washing by hand for a week?
- How does the mother tell her children that they'll have to make their own beds every day?
- How does the housewife say to her husband that they'll have to share the housework?
- How does the husband say to his wife that he has not time to do the housework?

Traditionally, household chores have been done by women. Mothers have been staying at home, for centuries, making the beds, dusting the furniture, doing the washing, going shopping, cooking, etc. They have always complained that their work was very badly paid, in fact, it was not paid at all. Then, after the Second World War, women started to go out to work for two reasons; first of all, because they didn't want to stay at home looking after children any more, doing the same boring jobs day after day; secondly, because the salary earned by the husbands was not enough to keep a family, or at least not with the high standard of living that people had got used to. If people wanted to have a house, a car, a fridge, a washing machine, TV set, etc, etc., obviously a high income was needed. Curiously enough, it sometimes happens that the husband is unemployed and has to stay at home looking after the children while his wife goes to work, and so the situation is reversed.

Questions

1. Who has always done the housework?
2. What other house chores can you think of?
3. What was the traditional complaint of women?
4. What happened after the Second World War?
5. Why do women go out to work?
6. What do women think of housework?
7. Can a family live on only one salary?
8. Why not?
9. What is curious about the new situation?
10. What does the wife do meanwhile?

Housekeeping

1. Are you a housewife?
2. Would you like to be one?
3. What do you think of working at home?
4. Do you think men should share in the housework?
5. Should women stay at home looking after the children?
6. What's the job you dislike most at home?
7. What's the job you like most?
8. What do you think of housework a hundred years ago?
9. How did they do the washing?
10. Did women go to work then?
11. What was your grandmother's life like?
12. Would you like to have many children?
13. How many children did women have last century?
14. How many children are you going to have?
15. Can a woman go to work if she has 8 children?
16. How did your grandmother clean the floors?
17. Did they have any hoovers?
18. Do you make your own bed?
19. Do you ever do the cooking?
20. What about the washing up? Do you like doing it?
21. Do you have a dishwasher?
22. Do you think it's worth having one?
23. What do you think of washing machines?
24. Have you ever washed a dirty handkerchief?
25. What would life be like without modern appliances?
26. Would you like to cook in the old pot hanging over the fire?
27. Have you ever lit a fire?
28. Can you describe how you light a fire in the fireplace?
29. What do you think of ironing?
30. How did people iron clothes before electric irons?
31. How would you make coffee the old way?
32. Have you ever darned woollen socks?
33. Do you know what a wooden egg is?
34. Do you have a fridge at home? a deep freezer?
35. What would you do without one?
36. Where did people keep food in the old days?
37. If you could keep only one appliance, which one would you choose?
38. If you were a man, would you stay at home while your wife went to work?
39. Should men go shopping?
40. Should they change the baby and do the washing up?

9 · Jobs

Glossary
self-employed
degree
successful
warder
to grow up
engine driver
later on
unemployed
training

Description of the scene:

Suggested roleplays and dialogues

· In pairs, act out the conversation between the personnel manager and a candidate for a vacancy.
· In pairs, act out the conversation between an unemployed person that goes to the Job Centre for the first time and the assistant.
· In groups, write down a list of jobs you can think of. The winner is the group that can write down most jobs.

Make comments on the following statements:

· What's the hardest job. Why?
· The job I would like to have.

· People may have to change jobs several times during their lifetime.
· There are many people unemployed in this country.

Questions on the scene

· What's the woman trying on?
· What's the girl doing on her knees?
· How would you describe the shop assistant's expression?
· How would you describe the customer's expression?
· Describe the shop.

True or false. Give reasons

· There are no large factories with thousands of workers nowadays.
· Many young people are self-employed.
· Public servants have jobs for a lifetime.
· Businessmen get a lot of money.
· Banks help people to set up small businesses.
· It's impossible to become rich working with your hands.

Questions based on language functions

· How does a woman customer say to the shop attendant that she wants to try on another dress?
· What does the assistant say to the customer when she has no more dresses to try on?
· How does an unemployed person ask for a job in a Job Centre?
· How does the attendant at the Job Centre say to this person that they haven't got a job for him/her?

If you ask the boys in a primary school what they would like to be when they grow up, most of them say engine drivers. Girls will say that they want to be film stars, or singers. Later on, when they are fourteen, they tend to be more realistic, although, most of them still haven't got a clear tendency towards one job or another.

The problem is that training for a specific kind of work takes such a long time, that, youngsters have to decide which path to take at an age in which most of them still don't know what they really like.

Many boys and girls find, when they are eighteen, that the work they are training for does not fulfil their expectations, and so, they have to start another kind of training, which is often quite different.

Not many years ago, people used to retire after being 40 years in the same job. Today, the average person will have to change jobs three or four times during his/her lifetime and spend several months unemployed between jobs.

Questions

1. What would boys in primary school like to be?
2. What about little girls?
3. What happens when they are fourteen?
4. Is training for a job easy?
5. How long does it take to train someone for a job?
6. When do youngsters decide which path to follow?
7. What happens very often when boys and girls are eighteen?
8. What do they have to do?
9. How long did people use to be in the same job?
10. How often do people change jobs during their lifetime?

Jobs

1. What do you do?
2. What would you like to be?
3. Are you studying for it?
4. Would you like to be self-employed?
5. What are the advantages and disadvantages of it?
6. Do you prefer to get a salary?
7. What are the advantages and disadvantages of it?
8. Have you ever been employed?
9. Is it difficult to get a job?
10. Which different jobs have you done?
11. What sort of jobs do you think are best?
12. What sort of jobs are the best paid?
13. What are the worst jobs?
14. What are the advantages and disadvantages of manual jobs?
15. What are the advantages and disadvantages of intellectual jobs?
16. What do you think of teachers? Would you like to be one?
17. Is it difficult to become a teacher?
18. What do think of business people?
19. Would you like to be one?
20. What's the best thing about being a businessman?
21. What's the worst thing about it?
22. Do you think that a university degree helps a person to be successful?
23. Can you become rich by working?
24. What do you prefer, to be rich or to have a good job?
25. Are you in favour of women working?
26. Do you think that housekeeping is a job?
27. How many hours does a housewife work?
28. Would you like to be a housewife?
29. What's your opinion of night work?
30. Have you ever been working all night?
31. How do you feel the next day?
32. Which are the advantages and disadvantages?
33. What do you prefer, an office job or to be out in the open air?
34. Can you describe your father's work?
35. What about your mother's work? what does she do all day?
36. Would you like to work in commerce/industry?
37. Describe the job of a shop assistant.
38. Describe the job of a person working in a factory.
39. Would you like to be a public servant: policeman, warder?
40. What's the difference between these two jobs?

10 · Military Service

Glossary

compulsory
firearms
unpleasant
regular
to earn
treated
parade
join
taught
pool
muddy
nappy
pot
to scrub
to abolish
burden
drill

Description of the scene:

Suggested roleplays and dialogues

- In pairs, act out a conversation between the sergeant and a recruit learning how to march.
- In pairs, act out a conversation between the instructor and a soldier learning how to fire a rifle.
- In groups, act out a conversation among several soldiers who are marching through the night with full gear.

Make comments on the following statements

- Women should do the military service.
- There should be a regular army in all countries.
- To learn how to use a rifle is a good thing.
- Professional soldiers should learn a trade.

Questions on the scene

- Is this the Army headquarters?
- Are the two boys that are cleaning up volunteers?
- How would you describe the sergeant's expression?
- Describe the uniforms of the sailors.
- Why do you think the two boys are cleaning up the place?

True or false. Give reasons

- In Britain everybody has to do the military service.
- A soldier can learn a trade in the regular army.
- In the regular army soldiers get a good salary.
- Learning to drive a tank can be very useful.
- In most countries people have to do the military service.
- Parachute Jumping is dangerous.

Questions based on language functions

- What does the sergeant say to the two soldiers if he wants them to clean the latrines?
- What do the soldiers say if they want to refuse?
- What does the captain say to the sergeant if he wants them to practise some drill?
- How does the sergeant say to the soldiers that they are going to do a night march?

The question is: should young men do military service? And if they should, why don't girls do it? Aren't women vindicating equality between men and women? If men and women are equal in all respects, women also have the same obligations. To learn to use the rifle lying down flat in a pool of muddy water, or marching with full gear through the night over the mountains will certainly make women hard and strong, quite prepared to face a future married life of nappy-washing and pot-scrubbing.

· On the other hand, there is a very strong movement towards abolishing the obligation to do military service. In fact, countries like Britain or Canada have for a long time done away with that burden. In the British Army, all soldiers, airmen and seamen are professional. This means that they are paid for the work they do and they make a career in the forces. Most countries claim that having a regular army is expensive. But it's far more expensive to have half a million young men wasting a year of their lives cleaning the latrines of the headquarters.

Questions

1. What's the first question the writer asks?
2. What does he say about girls?
3. What do women vindicate?
4. Should women have the same obligations?
5. What two things does the writer say soldiers do?
6. Can you suggest another one?
7. What sort of military service is there in Great Britain?
8. Are soldiers paid?
9. Why do many countries object to having a regular army?
10. What do soldiers do in the headquarters according to the writer?

Military Service

1. Are you going to do military service? When?
2. Do you think women should do military service?
3. Is military service compulsory in your country?
4. What are the advantages of doing military service?
5. What are the disadvantages?
6. Do you like firearms?
7. Where would you like to do military service? Army? Navy? Air Force?
8. What sort of things would you have to do in the Army?
9. What sort of things would you have to do in the Navy?
10. What sort of things would you have to do in the Air Force?
11. What is the most unpleasant part of military service?
12. How long is military service in your country?
13. What do you think of a regular army?
14. Do you think soldiers should be professionals?
15. Do you know of any country that has a regular army?
16. What are the advantages of a regular army?
17. What are the disadvantages?
18. How much do you think soldiers should earn?
19. Do you think soldiers are treated well by the officers?
20. Would you like being on parade?
21. Would you like to drive a tank?
22. Would you like to fire a machine-gun?
23. What's your favourite weapon?
24. What would you do if you had to fight against the other sex?
25. Do you like the infantry?
26. What do they do?
27. Would you like to parachute jump?
28. Do you think it's dangerous?
29. What sort of things can happen to a parachute?
30. Would you like to be a radio operator?
31. What do you think they do?
32. Do you think soldiers should learn a trade?
33. Would you join the army if they taught you something for your future?
34. Don't you think that everybody should do basic training?
35. What do you think of doing the military service in the summer?
36. Would you volunteer if your country was attacked?
37. What's the food like in the army?
38. Describe the food that you would like to eat there.
39. What do you think of people leaving food on their plates?
40. Do you think soldiers should have wine with their meals?

11 · Television

Glossary

meals
hinders
wonders
quiet
glue
digest
void
meaningless
jokes
unshameful
tears
choices

Description of the scene:

Suggested roleplays and dialogues

- In pairs, act out the conversation between the father and the child who are watching TV.
- In pairs, act out a conversation between a boy and a girl who want to watch different programmes.
- In groups, act out a conversation between the mother serving dinner and the children watching TV.

Make comments on the following statements:

- Advantages and disadvantages of TV.
- There shouldn't be any sex on TV.
- Watching TV during dinner/lunch is a good/bad thing.
- Having many choices of programmes is good/bad.

Questions on the scene

- Are the boys sitting?
- Is the father watching TV?
- What are the children watching?
- Have they got their slippers on?

True or false. Give reasons

- Television serials are boring.
- American films are difficult to understand for foreigners.
- Watching cartoons is a way of keeping the children quiet.
- Most families watch TV during meals.
- There's too much sex and violence on TV.
- There's too much advertising on TV.

Questions based on language functions

- What does the mother say to the children if they are watching too much TV?
- What do the children say if they refuse to switch off the TV?
- What does the husband say to the family if he wants to watch a football match on TV?
- What does the wife say if she doesn't want to see the football?

'Magic square box', that's the name by which television is known by many people. It works wonders in keeping children quiet. Just put on some cartoons and you have no children for two hours. Little boys and girls glue their eyes to the screen and seem to be hypnotized by the magic power of the little square box. They follow and digest, without a word, hundreds of the incredible adventures of Mickey Mouse, Penélope or the fantastic Japanese space heroes.

But not only children are captivated by television. Most grown ups sit in front of the screen for four or five hours a day. Life without television would be void and meaningless for them. Millions of people laugh automátically at the standard jokes of the funny programmes, and then cry unshameful tears at the moving scenes of the never-ending South American serials.

The problem for many families is which channel to watch. In some countries there are a dozen choices. Very soon we'll have a hundred choices. What shall we do then? As for myself it's very clear; I'll go back to my old adventure books.

Questions

1. What's the name that people give to Television?
2. What does TV do to children?
3. What do children seem to be?
4. Which examples of cartoon characters does the writer give?
5. Give six more names of cartoon heroes.
6. How many hours a day do grown ups spend in front of the TV?
7. The writer mentions two things people do when watching TV, what are they?
8. How many channels can people usually watch?
9. How many channels will you be able to choose from, very soon?
10. What's the writer going to do when that happens?

Television

1. Do you watch a lot of TV? How many hours a day?
2. Do you think watching TV is good?
3. Which programmes do you like best?
4. How many channels are there in your country?
5. Do you think children should watch TV?
6. Do you like cartoons? Which cartoon do you like best?
7. Would you like to live in a place with no TV?
8. What would you do if you didn't have TV?
9. Which channel do you prefer? A local channel or a national one?
10. Do you have a satelite aerial? Can you watch films in English?
11. Are English films difficult to understand? And American films?
12. Are programmes good in your country?
13. What would you do to improve them?
14. Do you think TV should be subsidised by the government?
15. What do you think of advertising on TV?
16. Would you be willing to pay a monthly fee in order not to have ads?
17. Are private channels better than state controlled channels?
18. Do you like watching the news on TV?
19. Do you watch TV during meals?
20. Do you think TV helps or hinders family unity?
21. What do you think of children who watch TV before going to school?
22. Is TV a good thing to keep children quiet?
23. Do you think TV should substitute family games?
24. What do you think of long TV serials? Do you watch them?
25. What sort of programmes are popular in your country?
26. What do you think of sex on TV?
27. Do you think children should watch sex?
28. What about violence? What do you think of it? Do you like it?
29. Do you think children like it? Is it good, bad, or indifferent for them?
30. What's better, to read books or to watch TV?
31. Can you do both?
32. Which is better for learning?
33. If you were the TV controller what type of programmes would you put on, in the mornings?
34. What about the afternoon programmes?
35. And in the evening?
36. Do you agree with sex films after midnight?
37. What are the possibilities of education on TV?
38. Give advantages and disadvantages of TV.
39. Were people happier or more unhappy before TV?
40. What will TV be like in the future?

12 · Christmas

Glossary
crib
look
forward
food
fellow
citizens
birth
peace
lay down
to feel
warmer
truce
bitter
barbed wire
bullets

· What's the old man doing?
· What's the weather like?
· What's on the floor?
· What's there on the background of the picture?

True or false. Give reasons

· Father Christmas exists only in the imagination.
· In South America they spend Christmas on the beach.
· In some countries the three wise men are the ones that bring the presents.
· In Britain Boxing Day is the day after Christmas.

Questions based on language functions

· What do children say to their mothers if they want to write to Father Christmas?
· What do parents say to their children if they've been naughty?
· What does Father Christmas say to the children if he sees them in the street?
· What do people say to each other at Christmas?

Description of the scene:

Suggested roleplays and dialogues

· In pairs, act out a conversation between the father or mother and a small child who wants to write to Father Christmas.
· In group, act out a conversation at dinner time on Christmas day.
· In pairs, act out a conversation between two enemy soldiers during the First World War on Christmas day.

Make comments on the following statements:

· Father Christmas brings presents to children that have been good.
· He brings coal to children who have been naughty.
· People go singing carols round the houses.
· If Christmas didn't exist it should be invented.
· Children are given too many presents at Christmas.
· We all eat and drink too much at Christmas.
· Christmas should be celebrated in summer.

Questions on the scene

· How many children are there singing?
· How many people are listening to them?

Somebody said once that if Christmas didn't exist it should be invented. Why did he say that? Well, any sociologist could tell us that we all occasionally need a time in which to put aside our frantic daily activities and relax. Christmas time is not only a time for relaxing but also a time in which we are all more inclined to love our fellow citizens. The celebration of the birth of Jesus brings us the idea of peace and tranquility. It's a time in which all human beings tend to be at peace with other people. At least once a year we lay down our arms and feel warmer towards our enemies. My grandfather used to tell me that during the First World War, Christmas Day was a day of truce. Not a single shot was fired at the enemy. In some places a football match was organized between the bitter enemies, and there, in the middle of no man's land, and pulling the barbed wire to one side, the ground was cleared for twenty-two men to settle their differences with a ball instead of bullets. It was the Christmas spirit.

Questions

1. What did somebody say once?
2. What do we need occasionally?
3. How do we feel at Christmas?
4. What does the celebration of Christmas bring to us?
5. What is the tendency at that time?
6. What should we do at least once a year?
7. What did the writer's grandfather use to say?
8. Was the enemy shot at on Christmas day?
9. What happened in some places?
10. How did the soldiers settle their differences?

Christmas

1. What do you do on Christmas day?
2. Which do you prefer Chirstmas Day or Christmas Eve?
3. At what time do you go to bed on Christmas Eve?
4. What do you do on Christmas Eve?
5. Do people go singing carols round the houses or shops?
6. Have you ever done it? If not, why not?
7. What do people do in your country on Christmas Eve?
8. What time do pubs close on Christmas Eve in your country?
9. What do you like most about Christmas?
10. Do you give many presents at Chirstmas?
11. What presents did you get last Chirstmas?
12. What day do you get your presents?
13. Do you decorate your house?
14. Do you put up a crib or a Christmas tree?
15. Did you look forward to Xmas when you were little?
16. Do you still believe in Father Christmas?
17. When did you discover the truth about Father Christmas?
18. What do you do during the Christmas holiday?
19. What food is typical at that time of the year?
20. Do you drink at home? What do you drink?
21. Do you write to Father Christmas?
22. What would you like to get this year?
23. Which do you prefer, toys, games or clothes?
24. When do schools start again after the New Year?
25. How do you feel when you go back to school/work?
26. What sort of weather do you usually have?
27. Would you like to spend Christmas on the beach?
28. What do children get in your country when they've been naughty?
29. Do parents like playing with children's toys?
30. What do children do with expensive toys?
31. What was your favourite toy? Was it expensive?
32. What do you think of educational toys?
33. In which part of the world is December the hot season?
34. What do you like at Christmas?
35. What don't you like at Christmas?
36. Would you like to spend Christmas away from home? Why not?
37. Do all countries celebrate Christmas? What countries don't celebrate it?
38. What do we celebrate on Christmas Day?
39. Do you know what Boxing day is? Do you have that in your country?
40. Are you sorry when Christmas is over?

13 · Driving

Glossary
drive
carelessness
seat belts
helmets
to brake
safe
in order to
gadgets
smoothly
stretched
straight
to
straighten
kerb
yanked
steering
wheel
aimed for
embankment
to scream
angrily

Description of the scene:

Suggested roleplays and dialogues

· In pairs, act out the conversation between the instructor and the woman.
· In pairs, act out the conversation between the instructor and the learner in Smith's driving school.
· In a group, talk about your experience as a learner.

Make comments on the following statements:

· Women are very bad drivers.
· 16 is a good age to drive a car.
· Drunken drivers should lose their driving licence.
· Drivers should wear safety belts and motorcyclists helmets.

Questions on the scene

· How would you describe the instructor's expression?
· What sort of manoeuvre is the learner doing?
· What happened to the tree behind Taylor's car?
· What do you think the instructor is telling the woman?

True or false. Give reasons

· Speed limit in town is 100 m.p.h.
· Women drivers are more dangerous than men according to statistics.
· Learning to drive is expensive.
· Most accidents are caused by drivers' carelessness.
· Boys and girls can drive at the age of 16 in America.

Questions based on language functions

· What does the instructor say to the learner that has to start the car?
· How does the learner say to the instructor that he doesn't remember how to start it?
· How does the instructor say to the learner that he has to put on the seat belt?
· What does the learner say to the instructor if he doesn't remember how to stop the car?

After Mr Jenkins had taught his four sons and daughters to drive, he thought that it would be a good idea to teach his wife. Mrs Jenkins was very enthusiastic about it. Early one Saturday morning, Mr Jenkins took the car to an old deserted road. After explaining to his wife the different functions of the gadgets in front of him, he changed seats with his wife. The engine was running smoothly, he put it into first gear for her and the car started to move forward gently. The road stretched for two hundred yards in a straight line. However, the car soon headed for the pavement on the right hand side. Just before hitting the kerb, Mr Jenkins managed to straighten the car despite his wife's opposition. Then, almost immediately, the car headed for the left kerb. Mr Jenkins again yanked the steering wheel just in time to prevent the bump. This time the car aimed for an embankment on the right hand side. 'Stop!', said Mr Jenkins. The car moved on. 'Stop, the car!' said Mr Jenkins louder. The car still went on. 'Stop it!' screamed Mr Jenkins as he pulled the hand brake up. The car stopped five inches from the embankment. 'Don't you shout at me', said Mrs Jenkins angrily to her perspiring husband. 'The trouble with you is that you have no patience.'

Questions

1. Whom did Mr Jenkins teach to drive?
2. What did he think would be a good idea?
3. Where did he take his wife?
4. What did he explain to his wife?
5. Why did they change seats?
6. What did he do when his wife sat in front of the controls?
7. What did the car do?
8. Did the car hit the right kerb?
9. What did the car do then?
10. What did Mr Jenkins do before the car hit the left kerb?
11. Where did the car head for, this time?
12. What did Mr Jenkins tell his wife?
13. What did Mr Jenkins say the second time?
14. What did Mr Jenkins do to prevent the car falling down the embankment?
15. What did Mrs Jenkins say?

Driving

1. Can you drive?
2. When did you learn? At what age?
3. Who taught you?
4. Where did you go to practise?
5. Which car did you use? What make was it?
6. Did you pass your driving test the first time?
7. Which part of the test did you fail?
8. Is the written part difficult?
9. What sort of questions do you get in the written part?
10. What manoeuvres did you have to do in the practical part?
11. Which one do you find most difficult?
12. Would you like to work as a driving instructor?
13. Do people get nervous when learning to drive?
14. Do you think driving is dangerous?
15. What do you do if the car in front is from a driving school?
16. At what age can you learn to drive in your country?
17. At what age can peple drive in America? (16)
18. Do you agree with the idea of people driving so young?
19. Do you think people should learn some mechanics?
20. What do you think of women drivers?
21. Are women better or worse drivers than men?
22. Do women take longer to learn to drive than men?
23. Which is more dangerous, to go fast, or to go too slow?
24. Do you create dangerous situations if you go too slow?
25. What do you think of speed limits?
26. Do people keep to these speed limits?
27. Are roads dangerous in your country?
28. Why are they?
29. What are accidents caused by, road conditions or drivers' carelessness?
30. Which are more dangerous, motorcycles or cars?
31. What do you think of seat belts? Are they of any use?
32. What about helmets? Are they of any use?
33. Is it safer to travel by motorway?
34. Can you describe an accident you saw?
35. Is it dangerous driving in the rain? Why?
36. Why doesn't a car come to a stop at the same distance when it is wet?
37. If the road is icy, would you brake hard in an emergency? What would happen if you did?
38. Are seat belts always safe? In which cases aren't seat belts safe?
39. Is an expensive car safer than a cheap one?
40. What items would you like your car to have in order to be safer?

14 · Travelling

Glossary
hitch-hiking
to cruise
trekking
choose
balloon
sleigh
lone
to recall
waggons
to stock
furnaces
coal
boiler
scrap yard
raw materials

Description of the scene:

Suggested roleplays and dialogues

- In a group of three, act out a conversation between the guide and the boy and girl.
- In pairs, act out a conversation between the shop assistant in an Indian shop and a tourist.
- In pairs, act out a conversation between a client at the travel agency and the assistant.
- In pairs, act out a conversation between the airhostess and a nervous traveller who is flying for the first time.

Make comments on the following statements:

- Flying is the safest way of travelling.
- Walking across the continent is the best way to see the world.
- Travelling first class is the same as travelling tourist.
- Hitch-hiking.

Questions on the scene

- How many camels are there?
- Describe the people riding the camels.
- Where are they going?
- What do you think the weather is like?

True or false. Give reasons

- Flying is the safest way of travelling according to the statistics.
- Many young people hitch-hike across the continent.
- Most people travel in summer.
- Many people travel abroad for their holidays.

Questions based on language functions

- What does a boy say to a girl if he wants her to accompany him cycling across the continent?
- What does the girl say to refuse his invitation?
- How does the husband say to his wife that they have won a trip to the Canary Island for two people?
- How does the wife say that she doesn't want to go?

Ryszard Walessa boarded the plane in New York and a few hours later he was talking business with a client in London. That very afternoon he was dining in Rome with a supplier of raw materials for his electronic equipment firm. Mr Walessa was now an executive, and he could permit himself these luxuries. Nevertheless, it was not always like this. In his young days the travelling he did had been quite different. He couldn't help a bitter smile when he recalled as a Polish refugee, after the war, he had crossed half of Europe hidden in trucks or empty railway waggons. Then, his life as a sailor came to his memory. Sailing as a fireman, stoking the furnaces with coal to keep up the pressure in the boiler of an ancient Panamanian cargo ship, which was on its last voyage to the scrap yard in Genoa. After that, he remembered working as an engineer on an old Swedish tanker that was crawling its way on an endless voyage to the Persian Gulf. Yes, travelling in those days was certainly different.

Questions

1. What was Walessa's nationality?
2. Where did he take the plane?
3. Where did he go to from New York?
4. Where did he go to from London?
5. What sort of firm did he have?
6. What was Mr Walessa now?
7. What was he after the war?
8. How did he travel across Europe?
9. What was his job on the Panamanian cargo ship?
10. What did he do on the Swedish tanker?

Travelling

1. Do you like travelling?
2. Have you ever been out of the country?
3. Which countries have you visited?
4. Which way do you like to travel?
5. Do you like flying? Aren't you afraid?
6. What do you think of hitch-hiking? Have you ever done any?
7. Have you made long journeys by train?
8. What do you think of a cruising holiday?
9. Would you like to spend your holidays trekking?
10. Do you like travelling alone or with other people?
11. What sort of company would you choose to go with you?
12. What do you think of people who walk around Europe?
13. Do you read much about famous journeys? Do you remember any?
14. Do your friends like travelling?
15. Which vehicle would you choose to go around Europe?
16. How would you like to cycle across the continent?
17. Would you like to go yachting in the Mediterranean?
18. Have your parents done much travelling?
19. Do they tell you stories about their journeys?
20. What about your grandfather? Did he travel much?
21. Have you read Gulliver's Travels?
22. What do you think of it? Do you think they are true stories?
23. Would you like to travel in a balloon?
24. What's the safest way of travelling?
25. Which is the most unpleasant way of travelling?
26. Which is the fastest way of travelling?
27. Would you like to travel by submarine?
28. Do you like making long journeys by car?
29. What countries would you like to visit if you had money?
30. Would you like to cross the desert in a jeep?
31. What about going through the jungle on an elephant?
32. Would you like to see the pyramids of Egypt?
33. What do you think of travelling to the North Pole?
34. Would you like to drive a dog sleigh?
35. Have you ever flown?
36. What did you think the first time you flew?
37. If you were rich, how would you like to travel?
38. Would you like to have a yacht?
39. Would you like to take part in a yachting competition around the world?
40. Would you like to be a lone sailor, travelling from place to place?

15 · Learning a foreign language

Glossary

foreign
boring
to amuse
widely
to get mixed up
to regard
brain
approach
blank
to record
aloud
to agree

Suggested roleplays and dialogues

· In pairs, act out a conversation between your language teacher and yourself.
· In pairs, act out a conversation between a Language School secretary and a person who wants to learn a language.
· In pairs, act out a conversation between two students as they leave the language school.

Make comments on the following statements:

· Learning languages is easy.
· A language should be taught all the time in that language.
· More people speak English than any other language.
· A language can be learnt by yourself.
· The best way to learn a language is...

Questions on the scene

· How many people are there in the picture?
· What are they doing?
· Which method is the man following?
· How many dictionaries can you see?
· Are they sitting or standing?
· What's he got on his head?
· What's the man doing?
· How would you describe the expression on his face?
· How would you describe the boy's expression?

True or false. Give reasons

· Children find it easy to learn a language.
· Writing Chinese is easy.
· Foreign languages are taught in most schools.
· Many boys and girls go as 'au pairs' to learn languages.
· Hotel receptionists must be able to speak several languages.
· English is the language that is most widely spoken in the world.

Questions based on language functions

· How does the teacher tell the student to do some reading?
· How does the student say that he can't speak; he has a sore throat?
· How does the teacher tell the class to repeat the Vocabulary with him/her?
· What does the student ask his teacher if he doesn't hear him/her?

What's the best age to learn a foreign language? That's the question that mothers often ask language experts. The answer, of course, is that a language should be learnt as early in life as possible. The earlier a child starts learning it the better. The next question is, how should a child learn a foreign language? Most teachers agree on that point. They say that a child should learn playing. He should regard the act of learning as a game. Playing games, singing songs and repeating aloud whole sentences is a very easy way of teaching a little child. It's incredible the retentiveness of a blank young brain. Whatever is recorded in it will be there for a lifetime.

Grown ups, on the other hand, need a different approach to learning. Things must be explained to them, especially grammar. They must learn the different grammar structures, must memorize the verbs and vocabulary. And in both cases the person learning a language should spend a good many months or years in the country whose language he is learning.

Questions

1. What's the question that mothers often ask language experts?
2. When should a language be learnt?
3. How should a child learn a foreign language?
4. Do teachers agree on that point?
5. Do children have a good memory?
6. Can grown ups learn the same way children do?
7. What's the difference?
8. What must grown ups memorize?
9. Where's the best place to learn a foreign language?
10. Should children be sent to this foreign country?

Learning a foreign language

1. How many foreign languages can you speak?
2. Which of the languages you know is the most difficult?
3. What do you think of the grammar?
4. Can you learn a language without grammar?
5. What's the most difficult part of learning a language?
6. Do you think grown ups can learn a language as children do?
7. Do you understand films in the original version?
8. Do you think that going to the country where the language is spoken is important?
9. How long should you stay in that country?
10. What do you think of spending a summer month in Great Britain?
11. What do you know about 'au pair' girls?
12. Can boys go as 'au pairs'?
13. What else can boys do in order to stay several months in a country?
14. Is it enough just to be in the country?
15. Do you think it is necessary to go to classes?
16. What do you think of reading? Does it help?
17. Can you learn a language by yourself?
18. What is the best age for learning languages?
19. How do children learn?
20. Is learning a language boring?
21. What would you do to amuse your pupils?
22. What's the most pleasant part of learning languages?
23. What's the most unpleasant part?
24. Should languages be taught at school?
25. Are languages important when looking for a job?
26. Which languages are most in demand?
27. How many languages should a secretary know?
28. What about a hotel receptionist?
29. What are the advantages of speaking languages?
30. If you want to travel what languages may help you?
31. What's the language most spoken in the world? (Mandarin)
32. What's the language most widely spoken in the world? (English)
33. Would you like to learn Chinese or Japanese? Why?
34. Are there many people in your home town learning these languages?
35. What would you have to do if you wanted to learn one of these languages?
36. How do you write Chinese? Left to right?
37. What about Arabic? How do you write it?
38. Do you think that children have difficulties when learning two languages at the same time?
39. Do you think they get mixed up?
40. What about adults? Do you think adults get mixed up when learning two languages at the same time?

16 · In a restaurant

Glossary
expensive
to drop
spoon
fork
table cloth
chop
to eat out
tip
custom
to fulfil
inner
deal
to carry out
treaty
work
miracles
quench
thirst

Description of the scene:

Suggested roleplays and dialogues

· In pairs, act out the conversation between the waiter and the customer.
· In pairs, act out a conversation between husband and wife after the waiter goes away.
· In pairs, act out a conversation in the kitchen between the waiter and the head waiter about the fly on the customer's plate.

Make comments on the following statements:

· Eating out is expensive.
· A waiter's job is very tiring.
· Giving tips is a good/bad habit.
· Food at a restaurant is better than at home.

Questions on the scene

· How many people are there in the picture?
· What's on the table nearest to us?
· How many people are wearing glasses?
· How many necklaces can you see?
· What has the waiter got in his hands?
· What's he going to do with it?

True or false. Give the reasons

· There's a fly on the lady's plate.
· This is an expensive restaurant.
· The waiter is wearing a tie.
· The customer is very angry.

Questions based on language functions

· What does the customer say to ask the waiter to bring another plate?
· What does the waiter say to apologize for the fly on the plate?
· What does the customer say to the waiter to ask him for the bill?
· How does the waiter ask the customer if they will have coffee?

My father used to say that restaurants are places where people go, not just to satisfy their appetites, but also to fulfil their inner desires to be served by others; to enjoy a good conversation in a relaxed atmosphere, and to exhibit good manners which are not often brought out at home.

The restaurant is the place where most business deals are carried out, most contracts are agreed upon, and most treaties are signed.

The well-being that a person feels when he or she has a full stomach, and the cheerfulness that two glasses of wine produce in a person's state of mind, work miracles in the solving of difficulties and the approach of different opinions to a problem.

Ever since man has walked on two legs, celebrations of all sorts have always been done at a table. Let a man quench his thirst and kill his hunger at your table and you've won half of the battle.

Questions

1. What did the writer's father use to say?
2. Are good table manners always exhibited at home?
3. What do people do at restaurants besides eating?
4. How does a person feel when s/he has a full stomach?
5. What does a glass of wine produce in a person?
6. Does that state of mind help to reach an understanding?
7. Where do celebrations always take place?
8. What should you do if you want to win over another person?
9. Can you have a relaxed conversation in a restaurant?
10. Why do business people take their customers to a restaurant?

In a restaurant

1. Have you ever been to a restaurant? Do you like eating in one?
2. What sort of restaurants do you have in your home town?
3. Have you ever been to a very expensive restaurant?
4. What would you do if you dropped a glass of wine on the table?
5. What would you do if your spoon or fork was dirty?
6. Do you like choosing from the Menu or do you prefer a fixed menu?
7. Do you like eating with a table cloth or without it?
8. If you had several forks and knives would you know which one to use?
9. Would you pick up a chop with your fingers?
10. What are the prices like in the restaurants in your home town?
11. How often do you eat out?
12. How do prices in your country compare with those in G. B.?
13. Do you like being served?
14. If the waiter made a mistake would you tell him?
15. Would you like to be a waiter/waitress?
16. What do you think of that job?
17. Do you give tips in restaurants?
18. What do you think of that custom?
19. What do you think of self-service restaurants?
20. Have you ever been to a free buffet?
21. Do you like the idea? What's a free buffet?
22. Are there many free buffets in your area?
23. What are the advantages of a self-service buffet?
24. Are there any disadvantages?
25. Do you think these restaurants get benefits?
26. What's better, a lot of food in a cheap place or little food in an expensive place?
27. What do you think of McDonalds, Burger King, etc.?
28. What are the advantages and disadvantages of these places?
29. Do you have 'Drive-in restaurants' in your country?
30. Where can you find them? What do you think of them?
31. Can you explain how you eat in these restaurants?
32. What sort of food can you expect in them?
33. What do you think of 'Gastronomic Societies'?
34. Do you have those in your country?
35. Where do you expect to find the best 'cuisine'?
36. What's the typical day to go to a restaurant?
37. Do you prefer to go at midday or in the evening?
38. What's the difference between a wedding banquet and a normal meal?
39. Which one do you prefer? Which is more expensive?
40. What do you think of Chinese food?

17· Success in life

Glossary
steps
successful
wealth
speech
nun
priest
salesman
agree
to mean
luck
to bring up
research
puzzling
handsome
struggle
to lie
to fail

Suggested roleplays and dialogues

- In pairs, act out a conversation between the chauffer and the rich man.
- In pairs, act out a conversation between the rich man and the woman.
- In pairs, act out a conversation between the rich man and the person he's going to see in the building.

Make comments on the following statements:

- Rich people are always very happy.
- The lady with the man is his wife.
- The chauffer is very happy with his job.
- Being a chauffer is hard work.

Questions on the scene

- What's the rich man wearing?
- What's the lady wearing?
- What sort of car do you think that is?
- What's the chauffer wearing?
- Are the buildings very tall?
- Is there a special name for very high buildings?
- How old do you think these people are?
- Where do you think they are going?

True or false. Give reasons

- All writers are successful.

Description of the scene:

- Success is a matter of luck.
- Possitive thoughts have a lot to do with success.
- It's very difficult for a pessimist to be successful.
- Memory can be improved by exercises.

Questions based on language functions

- What does the rich man say to the chauffer if he needs the car in half an hour?
- How does the chauffer say to the rich man that he can't leave the car in there for half an hour?
- How do you think the receptionist of the hotel will receive the rich couple?

Some people are successful while many others are not. Some people spend their lives trying to obtain something from life, but never get it, while others seem to convert everything they touch into gold?

Experts say that success in life has nothing to do with intelligence, education, memory or surroundings. A lot of research has been done in this field to find out why a man or a woman is successful. The results have always been puzzling.

Many successful people received a good education, others received none at all. Some are intelligent, others are not. Some are handsome, some are not.

On the other hand, two people who received the same education, who have similar intelligence, and who are getting the same opportunities in life, will never reach the same level of success. Very often one will succeed while the other will struggle through life.

The answer lies, according to experts, in self-confidence. The person who believes in himself will succeed, while the person who is not confident in his/her own capability will certainly fail.

Questions

1. Is everybody successful?
2. Has success anything to do with intelligence?
3. Has it anything to do with education?
4. Has any research been done in this area?
5. Has success anything to do with being good looking?
6. What are the results like?
7. Will two people with the same opportunities be equally successful?
8. Where does the answer lie?
9. Who will succeed?
10. Who will not succeed?

Success in life

1. Would you like to be successful in life?
2. What steps do you have to take to be successful?
3. In which walk of life would you like to be successful?
4. When can a person be considered successful?
5. Is happiness related to success?
6. What about wealth? Is wealth proportional to success?
7. Do you think education will help you?
8. What sort of education?
9. Can an uneducated person be successful?
10. Do you know of any millionaire who never went to school?
11. What qualities are most important to succeed?
12. Can memory be improved?
13. Do you know of any method to improve it?
14. What about personality? Is it important?
15. What do you understand by personality?
16. Are the eyes of a person important?
17. What about speech? Is that important?
18. How should you speak?
19. Is diction important?
20. Do you think making people feel comfortable is important?
21. Do you think that a book can help you to be successful?
22. Would Teresa of Calcutta be considered successful?
23. What about a nun, or a priest? Are they successful?
24. What qualities must a salesman have to be successful?
25. Some people say that we are all salesmen. Do you agree?
26. For a writer to be successful, how many books must he write?
27. What about a film star, how many films does he/she have to be in?
28. Has health anything to do with success?
29. Which would you prefer, to be healthy, to be wealthy or to be successful?
30. Can you be all three?
31. Do you think success means hard work?
32. Can you be successful with little work?
33. Has success anything to do with luck?
34. People who win the lottery, are they successful?
35. Can you describe the word 'success'?
36. Has the country in which you live anything to do with success?
37. Would you be more successful in America?
38. Can an African tribesman be successful?
39. What about success in married life?
40. Could you be successful bringing up children?

18 · Hotels

Glossary
noisy
tips
bellboy
cheap
rates
to earn
blanket
heating
all over

Description of the scene:

Suggested roleplays and dialogues

· In pairs, act out a conversation between the waiter and the clients.
· In pairs, act out a conversation between husband and wife about what they are going to do after breakfast.
· In pairs, act out a conversation between a boy and a girl on holiday in the same place.

Make comments on the following statements:

· This hotel seems to be located on a holiday resort.
· Many waiters in this kind of hotel are really students working in summer.
· Life in a holiday resort hotel is very different from the life in a hotel in the capital.

Questions on the scene

· How would you describe the waiter's face?
· What's he carrying?
· What's he wearing?
· What time of the day is it?
· What are the birds flying over the sea called?
· What's the woman wearing?
· What are they going to have for breakfast?
· Where do you think they'll go afterwards?

True or false. Give reasons

· The couple staying at the hotel are newly married.
· The hotel seems to be good.
· There's probably a little sandy beach near the hotel.
· It's winter.
· The sun is shining.
· The coffee is very hot.

Questions based on language functions

· What does the waiter ask the clients?
· What do you think the woman replies?
· How does the man ask his wife to go for a walk?
· How do you think the waiter will explain the guests how to go to the beach?

36

The first time that I went to a hotel I was just a little boy. Probably it was not a very good one because my parents were far from rich, but the place seemed very luxurious to me. We even had hot water in the rooms. I remember that the toilet was in the corridor, but that was normal in those days.

Since that day I have been to thousands of different hotels all over the world. For me they have become a sort of second home. After forty years as a travelling salesman I must have stayed at every single hotel in my country.

Some of the hotels I've been to, were really pleasant, with thick carpets, a cocktail bar in the room, and a free buffet breakfast which included champagne and caviar.

On the other hand, some other hotels were really terrible. I remember one in which I had to ask for another blanket because I was cold, the room had no heating, and I had to pay for the use of the extra blanket.

Questions

1. How old was the writer the first time he went to a hotel?
2. Was it a good hotel?
3. Were his parents rich?
4. What did he think of the place?
5. Did they have hot water in the rooms?
6. What does the writer do for a living?
7. What do good hotels offer their clients?
8. What did the writer have to ask for in a bad hotel?
9. Why was he cold?
10. What did he have to pay for?

Hotels

1. Have you ever spent the night in a hotel?
2. How much do you pay for a night in a good hotel in your country?
3. Do you sleep well in a hotel bed?
4. Are hotels noisy?
5. What do you think of hotel breakfasts?
6. What about other meals, are they good or bad?
7. Do you like to have a TV set in your room?
8. Do you have to make your own bed in a hotel?
9. Would you complain if there was too much noise or the TV set was not working?
10. Which do you prefer, a big comfortable hotel, or a small one with a garden?
11. Would you like to spend a holiday in a hotel?
12. Would you like to work in a hotel?
13. What do you think of the work of a receptionist? What does he/she do?
14. Would you like to be cleaning rooms? What do you think of that job?
15. What other jobs can you do in a hotel?
16. Would you take tips if you were a bell boy?
17. What are the advantages of a good hotel?
18. What are the disadvantages compared with your home?
19. What's the difference between a hotel and a motel?
20. What about a hostel, what is it?
21. What's a 'chain' of hotels? Do you know any?
22. Which days of the week can you get 'cheap rates' in a hotel?
23. Are the prices of hotels always the same?
24. What sort of hotels change the prices?
25. Which months are prices higher? Why?
26. What do some hotels offer for old age pensioners?
27. When do they offer 'cheap rates' to old people?
28. What do you think of this idea?
29. How much do old people pay for a holiday in the Canary Islands?
30. Do you think hotels earn money charging these prices?
31. Does the Government contribute towards these holidays?
32. What attractions do you find in the holiday resort hotels?
33. Can you think of anything else to attract people to these hotels?
34. What's a hotel appartment?
35. What is a suite in a hotel? Is it cheap?
36. What sort of comodities can you find in a luxury hotel?
37. What does 'room service' do for you?
38. Would you like to spend your honeymoon in a hotel or in an appartment?
39. What would the advantages be?
40. And the disadvantages?

19 · At the bank

Glossary
account
saving account
draft
to draw
unpaid
I.O.U.
straight away
percentage
bearer
to cash
mortgage
shares
loan
higher
leasing
mates
to deal with
business
bill

Ask the class to make a comment on the following

- People get very high interest in a saving account.
- When writing a nominal cheque you should put the name of the person.
- You want to buy some shares. What do you do?
- Personal loans pay higher interest than mortgages.
- Suggested roleplays and dialogues
- In pairs, act out a conversation between the cashier and the client.
- In pairs, act out a conversation between the bank manager and a client who wants to open an account.
- In a group of three, act out a conversation between a couple who want to get a mortgage and the man at the bank.

Make comments on the following statements:

- To buy a house or a flat you need a mortgage.
- An I.O.U. and a cheque is the same thing.
- Many people pay with credit cards nowadays.
- The interest is higher on a personal loan than on a mortgage.
- to buy shares you have to go to the Stock Exchange.

Questions on the scene

- What's the client doing at the cashier's desk?
- What do you think the couple sitting on the right are doing?
- What's the cashier doing at this moment?
- What's the apparatus the cashier has next to him called?
- What do bank employees usually wear?
- What is around the cashier?
- Is the woman with her back to us an employee of the bank?

Description of the scene:

True or false. Give reasons

- A nominal cheque can be cashed by anybody.
- A cheque made out to the 'bearer' can only be cashed by a person called 'bearer'.
- If you can't pay the mortgage of a house, the bank will auction that house to get its money back.

Questions based on language functions

- What does a man who want to cash a cheque say?
- Does a bank manager have his own office?
- Do you have to write your cheques in the bank?
- Do cashiers pay cheques when there is not enough money in the account?
- Do bank employees earn a lot of money?
- Do bank employees get cheaper loans?

I remember in my school days one of my mates used to lend money to other boys to buy sweets. He used to get the money back on Saturdays with interest. Years later that clever boy became a banker.

Banks are places where people borrow money and pay very high interest on it, and places where they leave their savings and get very low interest for it.

The difference between the interest rate for lending and borrowing give bankers their benefits. These benefits are usually enormous.

Nowadays, most people have to deal with a bank. It is practically impossible to buy a house or a car without asking for help from the bank. Most houses are bought on a mortgage. This means that the bank buys the house for you and you pay the money back to the bank in small quatities every month. The trouble is that you pay about three times the amount of money the house costs.

The same thing happens with business people. They have to draw their bills on their clients usually at ninety days. The bank advances the money but charges interest on it.

Questions

1. What does the writer remember of his school days?
2. When did he get his money back?
3. What became of him?
4. Can you describe a bank?
5. What gives banks their profits?
6. Can you buy a house without asking for help from the bank?
7. How are most houses bought?
8. Do you pay back to the bank the same amount of money they paid for the house?
9. Do business people have to deal with banks?
10. Why do they?

At the bank

1. Have you got a bank account?
2. What sort of account can one open in a bank?
3. What's the difference between a current account and a savings account?
4. What sort of people usually have a current account?
5. What sort of people usually have a savings acount?
6. Do you know what a draft is?
7. What sort of people draw drafts?
8. What happens if a draft comes back unpaid?
9. What is a cheque?
10. What's a chequebook?
11. If you have a savings account, will they give you a chequebook?
12. What's the difference between a cheque and an I.O.U.?
13. If you send a draft payable in 60 days to the bank, will they give you the money straight away?
14. What percentage will the bank take?
15. What's the difference between a cheque crossed or uncrossed?
16. What's a nominal cheque?
17. What's a cheque payable to the bearer?
18. Who can cash this kind of cheque?
19. Can a cheque payable to the bearer be crossed? Who can cash it?
20. What is a transfer?
21. What is a house mortgage?
22. What rates do banks charge for a mortgage nowadays?
23. Can you buy shares in a bank?
24. Can you buy shares of another bank or company in your bank?
25. Where do you keep these shares?
26. What is a credit card?
27. Can you mention two credit cards used in your country?
28. What are the advantages of a credit card?
29. What are the disadvantages of a credit card?
30. What methods of payment do banks have with credit cards?
31. Do credit cards have limits?
32. Who fixes those limits? What do they depend on?
33. What is a personal loan?
34. Can anybody get personal loans?
35. Is interest higher on those loans? If so, why?
36. What are the interest rates on personal loans in your country?
37. What happens if you can't pay back a personal loan?
38. What happens if somebody can't pay back a mortgage?
39. What is a lease?
40. Can you get a lease through a bank?

20 · Pubs

Glossary
allowed
spirits
kinds of
bitter
a chat
under age
to be left
noisy
darts
prams
within
whatever

Description of the scene:

Suggested roleplays and dialogues

· In pairs, act out a conversation between the barman and a client.
· In pairs, act out a conversation between a drunkard and a barman who refuses to serve him another drink.
· In a group, act out a conversation among several friends who want to play a game of darts.

Make comments on the following statements:

· The British pubs are different from the rest.
· In America there are no pubs.
· Alcoholic people should not be allowed in pubs.
· Boys and girls under 18 should not be allowed to drink alcohol.

Questions on the scene

· Describe the face of the man on the left.
· What has the woman in her hand?
· What do you think the waiter is telling the drunkard?
· What is he going to do with him?
· Who is the man on the right talking to?
· Where has he got his hand?
· What sort of bottles are the ones on the top of the picture?

True or false. Give reasons

· In Britain the pubs are open until 2 o'clock in the morning.
· In Great Britain people under 16 are not allowed to drink in pubs.
· Drinks are very cheap in the U.K.
· You can have a good meal in a pub.
· You're allowed to take your drink home.
· You can't buy a bottle of wine in a pub.
· People can't smoke in pubs.
· You can get a cup of coffee in a pub.

Questions based on language functions

· What does a man say if he wants to have a beer?
· What does the barman say if he thinks the man is drunk?
· What does a man say to a woman if he wants to treat her to a drink?
· What does the woman say to the man to refuse his invitation?

A pub is an English institution. They don't have pubs in America, for example. An English pub is a place where people meet for a drink, a chat, a song or a game of darts. Pubs are usually very noisy places.

In a pub you can drink beer and spirits: whisky, brandy, etc., but you can't always get a cup of coffee or tea. If you want those you have to go to a café.

Something peculiar about British pubs is that nobody under age is allowed inside. Even babies in prams have to be left outside, or go to a separate children's room.

Another thing which is very curious about pubs is the opening times. Until recently, they opened between eleven and two, and between eight and eleven p.m. Closing must be punctual. No drinks will be served after eleven o'clock, and whatever you have in your glass must be drunk up within five minutes.

Questions

1. What is a pub?
2. Are there pubs in America?
3. What do people do in pubs?
4. What do you drink in pubs?
5. Is anybody allowed in a pub?
6. At what time do pubs open?
7. At what time do they close?
8. Are pub landlords punctual at closing times?
9. Can you have a drink after eleven o'clock?
10. What must you do with your drink after eleven o'clock?

Pubs

1. Have you ever been to a pub?
2. Are the under 18 year olds allowed to go into a pub?
3. What can you drink in a pub?
4. Can you ask for coffee or tea in a pub?
5. Can you sing in a pub?
6. What games can you play in a pub?
7. What game is very typical in an English pub?
8. Would you like to work in a pub?
9. What would the working hours be?
10. Give any advantage of working there.
11. Give any disadvantage of working there.
12. Can you have a meal in a pub?
13. Compare the pubs in your country with those in the U.K.
14. What do people drink most in your country?
15. Do you think that pubs should be open all night?
16. In G.B. people under 18 are not allowed to drink liquor. What do you think?
17. Are there many alcoholics in your country?
18. Are there any alcoholic societies?
19. Should alcoholic people be allowed in pubs?
20. Why do people drink spirits?
21. What are the advantages of drinking?
22. What are the disadvantages of drinking?
23. Is there an area of pubs in your home town?
24. What sort of people go to this area?
25. Is there any difference between a pub and a bar?
26. In G.B. pubs are often divided into two parts. Can you explain the difference?
27. Can you buy a bottle of wine to take home in an English pub?
28. Are drinks expensive in the U.K.? Why?
29. Compare the prices of wines and spirits in your country with those in the U.K.
30. What's your opinion of the taxes?
31. Do you think people should be allowed to smoke in pubs?
32. Do you think drinking is a sort of addiction?
33. Is alcohol a drug? A hard drug or a soft drug?
34. Why do people go to pubs?
35. In G. B. pubs close early, at what time?
36. What are the opening hours of a pub in the U.K?
37. What do you have to do with your drink at closing time?
38. Are you allowed to take it home?
39. Do you know what Guiness is? Do you have it in your country?
40. What about other kinds of beer? Do you have bitter, lager, light ale, brown beer in your country?

21 · At the Doctor's

Glossary
to be right
to be wrong
pills
side effects
Health
Insurance
blood
X-ray
illness
pressure
to lead
faith
nevertheless

Description of the scene:

Suggested roleplays and dialogues

· In pairs, act out a conversation between the nurse and the old woman.
· In pairs, act out a conversation between the young man and the doctor.
· In pairs, act out a conversation between the doctor and the nurse about the people outside.

Make comments on the following statements:

· Doctors often prescribe 'placebos'.
· Doctors' writing is difficult to understand.
· Many people have psycological illnesses.
· High blood pressure is dangerous.
· Many doctors are heavy smokers.
· Medicines are very expensive.
· X-rays are dangerous.

Questions on the scene

· What is wrong with the man?
· What do you think is wrong with the old woman?
· The woman on the right, is she the doctor?
· What do you think she is asking the old woman?
· What's the picture on the wall inside the room?
· What's the old woman carrying?

True or false. Give reasons

· Medicines often have side effects.
· Doctors recommend not to smoke.
· X-rays are dangerous for health.
· High blood pressure is good for you.
· A man suffering from the heart has to do a lot of exercise.
· People who have suffered heart attacks follow a special diet.
· Doctors often make mistakes.

Questions based on language function

· What do you say to the doctor if you don't feel well?
· What does the doctor say to the patient if he has to examine his chest?
· What does the patient say to the doctor if he/she wants some aspirins?
· What does the doctor say to a patient to refuse to give him/her pain killers?

What do doctors have that makes them feel so important? Is it that they consider themselves important because they cure people?

But, do they really cure people? That's the question. What percentage of people really get cured by the green pills given to them by their doctors? Wouldn't most of them have got better without the pills? There are medicines called «placebos». These medicines are inoffensive pills with no medical effect at all. Nevertheless, people get cured the same as with the other pills. What is it then, that cures people? Many experts say that it's the faith patients have in their doctors. Many years ago there was a doctor that cured people just by listening to their problems and then making them repeat to themselves a hundred times a day: «I'm better. I'm getting much better.» After several weeks, in fact, most patients got much better.

Questions

1. Do doctors think they are important?
2. Why?
3. Do they really cure people?
4. What colour are the pills given to patients by doctors?
5. What's the name of the inoffensive pills with no effect at all?
6. Do they cure people?
7. What really cures these people?
8. How did a doctor cure his patients many years ago?
9. What did he make his patients do?
10. Did the patients get better?

At the Doctor's

1. Have you ever been to a doctor?
2. When do people go to the doctor?
3. What's your opinion of doctors?
4. Do you think they are always right?
5. Do you know of any cases in which they were wrong?
6. Do doctors prescribe a lot of medicines?
7. Are you taking any pills or tablets?
8. Have pills any side effects? Which ones?
9. What do you think of the Health Insurance in your country?
10. Are medicines free in your country?
11. What percentage do you pay of the cost of the medicines?
12. Do you understand the prescriptions?
13. Do you have to pay doctors in your country?
14. Are there any private Health Insurance Companies in your country?
15. Why do doctors recommend not to smoke?
16. Have you ever seen a doctor smoking?
17. What is worse smoking or drinking?
18. Do you usually have to wait long to see the doctor?
19. Have you ever had a blood test? What for?
20. Can you describe the experience?
21. Have you ever been X-rayed? Describe your experience.
22. Should a doctor be strict or kind with patients?
23. Have you heard of psychological illnesses?
24. What are they?
25. What are 'placebos'?
26. Have you heard of 'hypochondriacs' (people who always think they are ill)?
27. Has a doctor ever come to your house?
28. Was he/she in a hurry? Did he/she sit down?
29. Didn't you feel better as soon as he came?
30. What do you think of injections?
31. Where are injections usually applied?
32. What is blood pressure?
33. Do you know anybody who has high blood pressure?
34. What are the symptoms? What are the causes and the remedies?
35. What about low blood pressure?
36. What do you have to do if your blood pressure is low?
37. Do you know anybody who has had a heart attack?
38. What sort of life do they have to lead?
39. Do they have a special diet?
40. Can a person like that run a marathon?

22 · At the hospital

Description of the scene:

Suggested roleplays and dialogues

- In pairs, act out the dialogue between the patient and the visitor.
- In pairs, act out a conversation between the nurse and one of the patients.
- In pairs, act out a conversation between the nurse and the visitors.

Make comments on the following statements:

- Hospitals don't allow many visitors in the wards.
- Nurses look after the patients all night.
- Some relatives spend the night with the patients.
- When you're ill it's better to stay at a hospital.

Questions on the scene

- What have the patients in their arms?
- Describe the expression of the woman visitor.
- How many people are in the ward?
- Who do you think the couple standing are?
- What's the patient near the window doing?
- Who do you think the woman sitting is?

True or false. Give reasons.

- In all hospital wards there are TV sets.
- Visitors can walk in at any time.
- The doctors take the temperature of the patients.
- Nurses are very busy during the night.
- Hospitals have always existed.
- Maternity hospitals have decreased infant mortality.
- In some countries women give birth while working in the fields.

Questions based on language functions

- What does the visitor say to ask the patient is he's all right?
- What does the patient say if he's feeling well?
- What does the visitor say if she wants to ask the patient if he wants anything to read or to eat?
- What does the patient say to refuse her offer?

If you hear a siren in any city in the world the chances are that it is an ambulance taking an injured person to hospital. Hospitals are nowadays taken for granted; you feel ill, reach for your phone, and ten minutes later an ambulance rushes you to the emergency unit of the nearest hospital.

Nevertheless, we are lucky to be born in this century. Citizens of bygone years weren't so fortunate. Hospitals practically didn't exist until the Middle Ages, and it wasn't until late in the XIX century when organized care was taken of the wounded in wars, the injured in accidents or sick people.

Thousands of doctors and nurses work day and night in hospitals to provide 24-hour attention to patients completely free. National Health Insurance pays all the expenses.

Glossary
nurse
room mates
night duty
to wake up
to undergo
mistake
ward
the chances are
injured
to take for granted
to rush
bygone

Questions

1. if you hear a siren what will it probably be?
2. What do you do if you feel ill?
3. How long will an ambulance take to get to your house?
4. Where will the ambulance take you?
5. Why are we lucky to be born in this century?
6. When did hospitals begin to exist?
7. In what century did organized care become general?
8. Are there many doctors and nurses working in hospitals nowadays?
9. At what time do hospitals open?
10. Who pays for hospital care?

At the hospital

1. Have you ever been to hospital as a patient?
2. Why were you sent there? How long were you there?
3. Did you enjoy your stay in hospital?
4. Describe the nurses you had. What were they like?
5. Were you alone? Describe your room mates.
6. Did you have a TV set?
7. What was the food like?
8. Was the hospital clean?
9. What activities did you do?
10. Have you ever had an operation? Which one?
11. Were you anaesthetized? Describe how it was done.
12. Did the effects last very long?
13. Where did you wake up? How did you feel?
14. What are the visiting hours in your local hospital?
15. How many visitors can get into the room at the same time?
16. How do they control the number of visitors?
17. Do you think a patient likes to have visitors?
18. How many beds are there in every room?
19. Would you like to be a nurse in a hospital?
20. What jobs do they have to do?
21. Do doctors visit the patients very often?
22. What do doctors do in a hospital?
23. Are there any doctors on night duty in hospitals?
24. What do nurses do during the night?
25. Have you ever been to the Emergency Ward?
26. What sort of people go there? What cases did you see?
27. Are hospitals necessary? What happened in the old days?
28. When did hospitals begin to exist?
29. What are the hospital conditions in the Third World?
30. Can you imagine somebody undergoing the wrong operation by mistake?
31. What sort of operations are most common?
32. Can you imagine a person being operated on without being anaesthetized?
33. Why do doctors and nurses use a mask in an operating theatre?
34. What is an ICU? When do patients go there?
35. Can you visit people in that unit? Under what conditions?
36. What is a maternity hospital?
37. How were the babies born in the old days?
38. Has infant mortality decreased?
39. What is it due to?
40. How long have mothers got to stay in the maternity ward?

23 · Natural Medicine

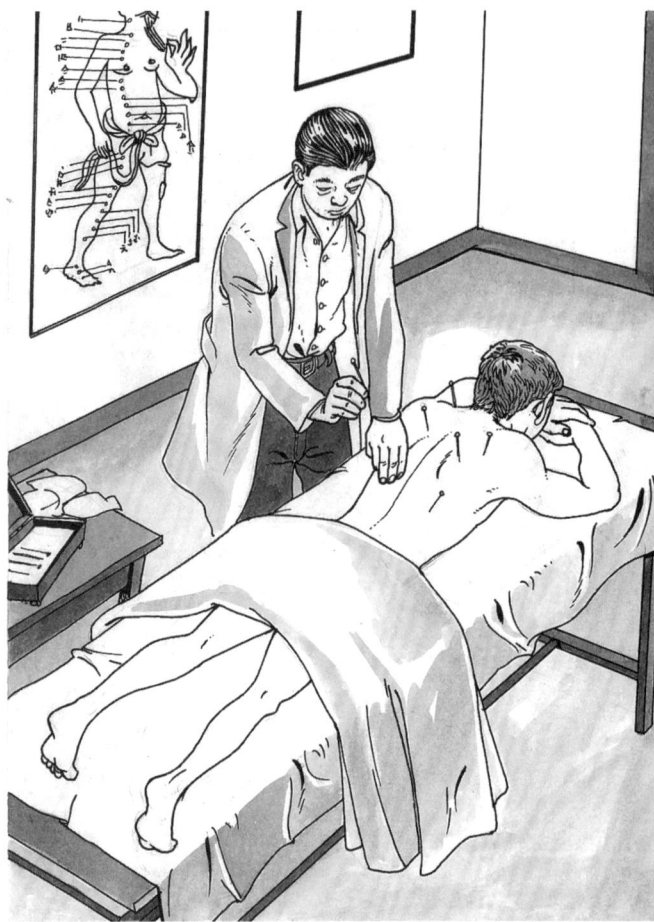

Glossary
whole rice
chance
healthy
to forbid
poison
power
brain
fashion
to seek
alleviate
aches
harm
faith

Description of the scene:

Suggested roleplays and dialogues

· In pairs, act out a conversation between the Chinese doctor and his patient.
· In pairs, act out a conversation between two friends. One has been to a magnetizer and the other to a macrobiotic naturist doctor.
· In a group, act out a conversation in which each student defends a different way of curing peeple.

Make comments on the following statements:

· Whole rice cures people.
· Some people give you energy with their hands.
· Some people operate with their bare hands.
· Some people never catch colds.
· Homeophaty is poison.
· Faith cures people.

Questions on the scene

· What nationality would you say the doctor is?
· Do you think the patient feels any pain?
· What's the effect of the needles in our body?
· Do you think these needles are all the same?
· What's the doctor wearing?
· What's the patient wearing?
· What sort of picture is there on the wall?
· How many needles are there in the box?
· How many are stuck in the patient's body?

True or false. Give reasons.

· Natural medicine has a lot of side effects.
· Most of the illnesses are psycosomatic (product of your head).
· Some religions don't allow people to eat pork.
· Water can cure.
· Some people never catch colds.
· People can be cured at a distance.
· Food has no influence on people's health.
· Colours have a lot of influence in our lives.

Questions based on language functions

· What do people do when they're ill?
· What do doctors usually prescribe?
· Do naturist doctors prescribe pills?
· Do you think food has anything to do with health?
· Do you think people should eat 'a little of everything'?
· Do you think that your thoughts can affect your health?

Natural medicine is in fashion. Millions of people, all over the world are very disappointed with traditional medicine. They find that the pills doctors give them have many side effects. In fact, quite often the remedy is worse than the cure. Then, many people go to seek natural remedies for their illnesses from naturist doctors or from people who can channel their energy to alleviate their aches.

Perhaps the best thing about natural medicine is that it has no side effects. People think that even if it doesn't cure, at least it doesn't do any harm.

Be it herbs, acupuncture, macrobiotics, homeopathy, the flowers of Bach or a thousand and one different ways of curing people, they are all effective - as long as the patient has faith in them.

Questions

1. What does the writer say about natural medicine?
2. Why do people go to naturalist doctors?
3. What is wrong with pills?
4. Is the remedy good?
5. What is best about natural medicine?
6. Does natural medicine do any harm?
7. Mention several different natural medicines.
8. How many ways of curing people are there according to the writer?
9. Are they effective?
10. What does the patient have to have?

Natural Medicine

1. What do you think of so called 'alternative medicine'?
2. Do you know a naturist doctor?
3. Have you ever been to one?
4. Why do they look in your eyes?
5. What sort of medicines do they give you?
6. Do these medicines have any side effects?
7. Has food any influence on people's health?
8. What is the Macrobiotic?
9. How does it cure you?
10. Can whole rice cure people?
11. How can you be cured eating cereals and vegetables?
12. Do you think that your own body can cure itself if you give it a chance?
13. Can vegetarians eat eggs or have milk?
14. What's the best way to keep healthy?
15. What's the difference between a vegetarian and a macrobiotic?
16. Some religions forbid eating pork and drinking alcohol, why?
17. Are there many ways of curing people?
18. What do you know about magnetism?
19. Have you seen people operating with their bare hands?
20. What's colour therapy? Can colour cure people?
21. What's rebirth? Do you think that that can help you?
22. What's acupuncture?
23. How does that help you?
24. Where does this therapy come from?
25. Have you heard of water therapy?
26. How can water help to cure illness?
27. Does saliva have any curing properties?
28. What do animals do?
29. Should you eat normally if you are sick? or injured?
30. Why do people catch colds?
31. Why do some people never catch colds?
32. Do people eat too much, too little or just right?
33. What is homeopathy? Are the little pills poison?
34. How can poison cure you?
35. Can people be cured at a distance?
36. Do you believe in mental power?
37. Do people use their brain power to the full?
38. Do you believe in 'energy'? Can we create energy?
39. The energy given out by magnetizers, is it their own energy?
40. If it's not theirs, where does it come from?

24 · Occultism

Glossary
death
to warn
fakes
evil
bare
tarpaulin
to splash
works

· What's on the table?
· What are they wearing?

True or false. Give reasons

· Two people can communicate by telepathy.
· An evil spirit can get inside a person.
· There's life after death.
· Some people use a crystal ball to see the future.
· Nobody believes in these things.

Description of the scene:

Suggested roleplays

· In pairs, act out a conversation between the medium and a client who wants to contact her dead husband.
· In pairs, act out a conversation between the medium and a spirit.
· In pairs, act out a conversation between two persons who are going to take part in a session of spiritism.

Make comments on the following statements:

· Energy can move objects.
· Voices of dead people have been recorded on tapes.
· Your future is written on your palm.
· Black magic or Voodoo can affect a person's health.
· A dead person sometimes 'comes back'.

Questions on the scene

· How many people are there in the picture?
· What are they doing?
· Which one is the medium?
· Why are they holding hands?
· Why do they have their eyes closed?

Questions based on language functions

· How does the customer ask the medium if she wants to communicate with a dead person?
· How does the medium invite the customer to take part in a session of spiritism?
· What does the medium say to refuse the customer's demand?
· How does the customer refuse the medium's invitation to take part in a session?

John Walker looked around the place. He had the feeling he had been there before. Yet, it was the first time he had visited that country.

Peter Redcliff could swear there was somebody in the room, he could feel a presence quite near him. Yet, he was alone.

Eddie Russell was jogging early in the morning. He passed near a tarpaulin placed horizontaly over some works. Suddenly the rainwater on the tarpaulin splashed down just behind him. He looked around but he was alone.

These are just three examples of strange things that happen to thousands of people all over the world every day. Some people say that these things are caused by spirits. Others suggest that we can cause things to move with the power of our minds.

As far as the first case is concerned, many people believe that we have all been here before, in other times, in other lives.

Occultism

1. Have you ever had a strange experience?
2. Have you ever had the sensation that you were not alone?
3. Have you ever had the feeling that you had already been somewhere before?
4. Have you taken part in a spiritism session?
5. Have you joined your energy with other people to move a glass?
6. Do you believe in those things?
7. Who do you think answers your questions?
8. Do you believe in spirits or life after death?
9. Have you heard voices of dead people being recorded on tapes?
10. Do you believe in telepathy?
11. Have you ever tried to send messages with your mind?
12. Do you know of any real cases?
13. Can spirits warn you of danger?
14. Have you heard of any cases in which that happened?
15. Do you think spirits can speak through people?
16. Are there any fakes in spiritism? Do you know of any cases?
17. Have you heard of a person who has just died appearing to a relative far away?
18. Have you heard of experiences of people 'coming back'?
19. How do these people feel?
20. Can spirits move objects?

Questions

1. What did John Walker feel?
2. Had he visited that country before?
3. What did Peter Redcliff feel near him?
4. Who was in the room with him?
5. What was Eddie Russell doing early one morning?
6. What happened when he passed near a tarpaulin?
7. Was there anybody near him?
8. What does the writer say about these examples?
9. Who or what causes these things according to some people?
10. What do other people suggest?

21. What's a Poltergeist?
22. Have you seen a film about it? What was it about?
23. Can an evil spirit get inside a person?
24. How can it be thrown out?
25. Do you think spirits have power over people?
26. Have you seen a person painting pictures of well known dead artists in four minutes?
27. Have you seen a person in a trance operate with bare hands in the name of a dead doctor?
28. Do you believe in 'black magic'?
29. What is 'Voodoo'?
30. Do you think 'Voodoo' can affect a normal person's life?
31. What's 'Tarot'?
32. What sort of cards are they?
33. How else can a clairvoyant predict the future?
34. Have you seen a crystal ball? Do you believe in it?
35. Do you think your future can be seen in the palms of your hands?
36. Can the future be changed?
37. Do you think your destiny is in the stars?
38. Can accidents be avoided?
39. What was a Pythoness in the old days?
40. Do you think many people believe in these things?

25 · Hypnotism-Telepathy

Glossary

whole
law
neck
circles
blindfolded
scrtach
to cheat
power
to the full
shifty
lain
heels
stiff
board
feat

Description of the scene:

Suggested roleplays
- In pairs, act out a conversation between the hypnotist and a client who wants to stop smoking.
- In pairs, act out a conversation between a hypnotist and a girl who is going to lay between two chairs.
- In pairs, act out a conversation between the hypnotist and a big man, in the audience, who is asked to sit on top of the hypnotized girl.

Make comments on the following statements:
- People that have been hypnotized don't remember anything.
- People can be hypnotized through television.
- Hypnotism can cure things.
- People do strange things when they are hypnotized.
- A man can drive a motorcycle blindfolded

Questions on the scene
- How many people are there on the scene?
- Who's the man in the picture on the wall?
- What has the man got in his hand?
- What's the man wearing?
- What's the woman wearing?
- What's she doing?

True or false. Give reasons
- Not everybody can be hypnotized.
- Bad habits, like smoking, can be cured with hypnotism.
- Objects can also be hypnotized.
- Electrical appliances can be repaired with the power of the mind.
- Thoughts can be transmitted from one person to another.

Questions based on language functions
- What does a woman say to a hypnotist if she wants help to stop smoking?
- What does the hypnotist say to send her to sleep?
- How does a woman say to a hypnotist that she wants to stop eating so much?
- What does the hypnotist ask her to do when she starts feeling hungry?

It is incredible what hypnotized people can do. I once watched, amazed, how a hypnotized young woman was laid across two chairs; her neck on the edge of one and her heels on the other. Her body was stiff, like a board, and three heavy men stood on her. For about two minutes she supported the weight of these people in that position. Of course, when she came to she didn't remember a thing. Where does a person get the energy to do such a feat?

Then, somebody among the audience wrote something on a piece of paper. The showman was able to read the mind of the person what he had written on the paper. That is called 'telepathy'. How can a person transmit his or her thoughts to another person?

Questions

1. What is the writer describing?
2. In what position was the young woman laid?
3. Where was her neck placed?
4. What about her heels, where were they put?
5. What was her body like?
6. How many men stood on her?
7. How long did they stand there for?
8. What did somebody in the audience do next?
9. What did the showman do?
10. What is the transmission of thoughts called?

Hipnotism-Telepathy

1. Have you been hypnotized?
2. What do you think of it?
3. Is hypnotism a good thing or a bad thing?
4. Can hypnotism cure something?
5. Do hypnotized people remember anything when they wake up?
6. Have you seen people being hypnotized? Describe what they did.
7. Can anybody be hypnotized?
8. Can you resist being hypnotized?
9. Can anybody be a hypnotist?
10. Do you have to learn anything to become a hypnotist?
11. Do hypnotists take advantage of their power?
12. Can hypnotism affect the whole audience of a theatre?
13. Can people be hypnotized through television?
14. What would happen if they couldn't 'come back'?
15. Do people change their chracter when they are hypnotized?
16. Can objects be hypnotized?
17. Can animals be hypnotized?
18. Can watches be repaired by the power of the mind?
19. What else can be done by the power of the mind?
20. Can hypnotized people do things that they can't normally do?
21. Could hypnotized people be induced to do things against the law?
22. Would you like to have this power over other people?
23. What do you have to do to become a hypnotist?
24. Have you tried concentrating your eyes on the back of somebody's neck?
25. Have you ever passed a message by telepathy?
26. Have you done the experiment of circles, stars and triangles?
27. How many of them did you get right?
28. Can a man drive a motorcycle blindfolded?
29. How can that be done? Is there a trick?
30. Does telepathy work with animals?
31. Can you order your dog to do something with your mind?
32. Have you ordered anybody to scratch his/her head with your mind?
33. Did he/she do it? Was it a coincidence?
34. If you could receive messages by telepathy, what benefits would you obtain from it?
35. Would you cheat in an exam? How?
36. What things could we do if we used our mind power to the full?
37. Can you see the character of a person by looking in his eyes?
38. A man with shifty eyes, will he have power in his mind?
39. Have you seen a man with such strong power in his eyes that you had to look away?
40. Do you think that strong will power can affect your social position?

26 · Collecting things

Glossary
mint stamps
auction
to invest
value
to print
postage
pastime
mat
radio set
dustbins

Description of the scene:

Suggested roleplays
- In pairs, act out a conversation between two people who collect dustbins and radio sets.
- In pairs, act out a conversation between a person who wants to start collecting stamps and a stamp dealer.
- In pairs, act out a conversation between old car collectors.

Make comments on the following statements:
- Many people like collecting things? Collecting stamps is the most popular collection.
- A little stamp may be worth a fortune.
- Some countries print stamps only for collectors.
- Little boys like to collect pictures of footballers.

Questions on the scene
- What's the man doing?
- What's has he got on the table?
- What's there on the shelf behind him?
- What's there on the shelf on his right?
- What's the man got in his right hand?
- What's he holding in his left hand?
- What's he wearing?

True or false. Give reasons
- Little girls collect pictures of footballers.
- Stamp collecting can be a good investment.
- All stamps are printed for postage.
- You can buy used stamps for collection at the Post Office.

Questions based on language functions
- What does the customer say to the stamp dealer if he wants to start a collection?
- What does the dealer say to the customer to inform him that the first thing is to buy a book with a picture of all the stamps of the country?
- What does a customer say to a dealer if he wants to invest money in stamps?
- How does the dealer suggest that he can buy a little stamp worth a million pounds?

Are you one of the collecting manics? It's incredible, but you'd be surprised at the number of people who collect things. Stamp collecting is, of course, the most common pastime, but there are thousands of all sorts of strange things that are collected by normal citizens like you and me. Some are very cheap like metal bottle tops, or little beer mats; others are expensive and difficult to find, like old radio sets; some others are really expensive like old cars.

A friend of mine collected dustbins. At the back of his house he had built a sort of greenhouse which was full of these containers, fortunately empty.

Another friend confessed he had a passion for collecting something that his wife didn't like at all. He liked to collect love letters from old girlfriends.

Questions

1. Are there many people who like collecting things?
2. Which is the thing that people collect most?
3. Mention two cheap things that can be collected.
4. What are the other things that can be collected, but are more expensive?
5. What sort of cars do some people collect?
6. What did a friend of the writer's collect?
7. Where did he keep the dustbins?
8. Were they full?
9. What would his other friend like to collect?
10. Why would his wife object?

Collecting things

1. Do you collect anything?
2. Does anybody in your family collect stamps?
3. Is it expensive to collect stamps?
4. Which is better, to collect used stamps or mint ones?
5. Have you heard of an expensive stamp? How much was it?
6. Is collecting stamps a good business?
7. What else can you collect besides stamps?
8. What's the strangest collection you've heard of?
9. What do boys usually collect?
10. What do little girls usually collect?
11. What do you think of collecting old cars?
12. What are the advantages of collecting things?
13. What are the disadvantages of collecting things?
14. Why do you think people collect things?
15. Can live animals be considered a collection?
16. What things can a rich Arab collect?
17. What can you collect on a beach?
18. Besides stamps, what is the second thing people collect most?
19. Is it difficult to sell a collection?
20. What is an auction?
21. Have you ever been to one?
22. What's the advantage of buying something in an auction?
23. What's the disadvantage of buying something in an auction?
24. Can collectors be considered strange people?
25. Can collecting things be considered a profitable investment?
26. Would you invest a million pounds in a collection?
27. Are there any stamp shops in your town?
28. Do you think the owners of the shops collect stamps?
29. If you want to sell your collection will they buy it?
30. Do you think they will pay well?
31. How else can you sell a stamp collection?
32. Who really makes profit of stamp collecting?
33. If you collect stamps what do you need to buy besides stamps?
34. Have all the stamps the same value once they've been used?
35. What makes some stamps so valuable?
36. Does the value depend on the paper quality?
37. Why do some countries print such a lot of stamps?
38. Are stamps printed only for postage reasons?
39. Are they printed for collectors only?
40. Have you heard of people who collect boyfriends/girlfriends?

27 · At the dentist

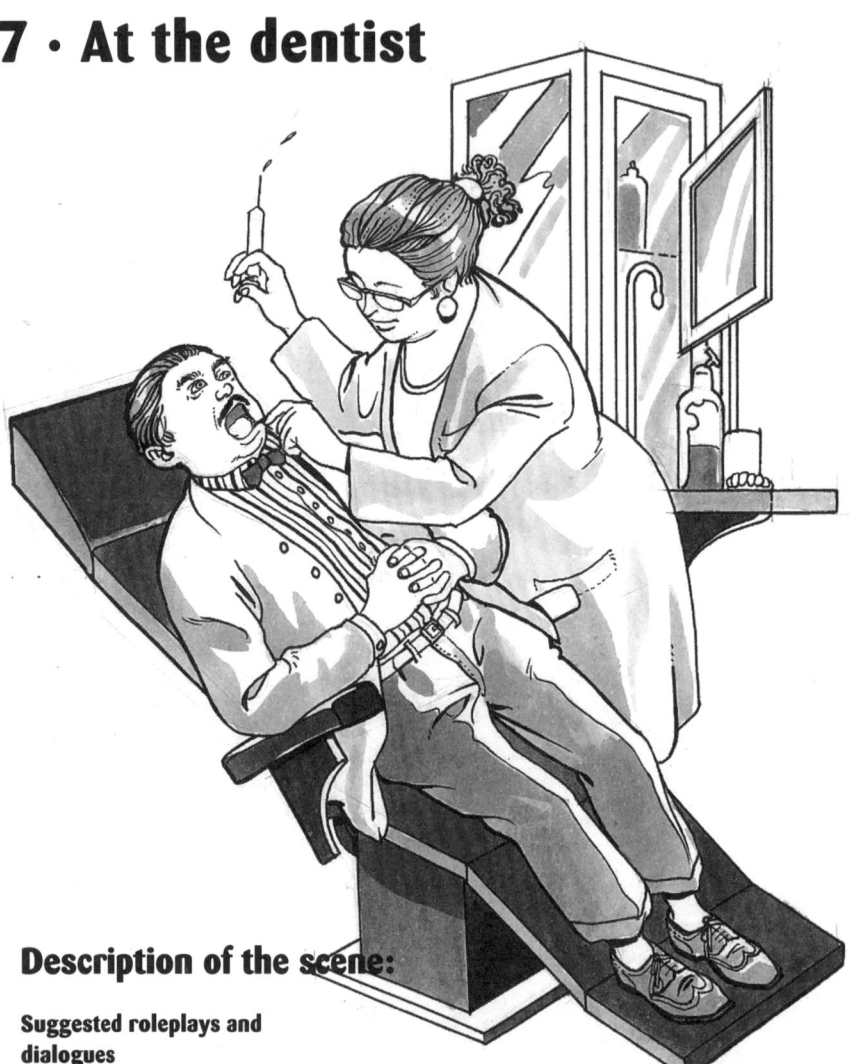

Glossary

fillings
to pull out
to fill
painful
numbed
dental floss
drill
breath
toothbrush
masochism
ordeal
decay
teething
thorough
to unwrap
to rush

Description of the scene:

Suggested roleplays and dialogues

- In pairs, act out a conversation between the dentist and the patient.
- In pairs, act out a conversation between husband and wife. The husband has toothache.
- In pairs, act out a conversation between two people in the dentist's waiting room.
- Commentaries on the following statements:
- People are afraid of going to the dentist.
- To have a tooth pulled out is painful.
- It's better to have a tooth out than to have it filled.
- Dentists should wear masks.
- You should clean your teeth three times a day after meals.
- Toothpaste kills all the bacteria.

Questions on the scene

- What has the doctor got in his hand?
- Describe the expression of the dentist.
- Is he wearing a mask?
- What is he wearing?
- What is he doing with his left hand?
- Would you say the dentist is young?
- Describe the patient's expression.
- What is he doing with his left hand?
- What is she wearing?

True or false. Give reasons.

- People eat too much sugar.
- Chocolate helps to keep the teeth healthy
- Film stars have such white teeth because they clean them regularly.
- White teeth are stronger than yellow teeth.
- Tobacco makes the teeth yellow.
- People that go to the dentists are all masochists.

Questions based on language functions

- What does the dentist tell you to do when you sit on the dentist's chair?
- What does a patient do when the dentist speaks to him and he has his mouth open?
- Do people go to the dentist very often?
- How often do you think people should go?
- What does the dentist tell you to do after he has been working

Most people consider that going to the dentist is a sort of masochism. It's one of the most unpleasant things that humans have to do in order to keep healthy. And however, we should undergo this ordeal at least once a year. Eating pre-packed food, rich in sugar, bacteria is permanently in our mouths, saliva and dentine. Dental decay affect practically 100% of the population and that includes childlren with their first teeth.

Dentists keep telling us to brush our teeth three times a day after meals and to do a thorough job of it, but who spends ten minutes brushing one's teeth after meals? As fas as I'm concerned I dedicate 30 seconds flat to such an important job before I rush out to catch the train to the office... while I unwrap a chocolate bar.

Questions

1. What's people's opinion about dentists?
2. Is it pleasant going to the dentist?
3. How often should people go to the dentist?
4. Why do people get a lot of dental decay nowadays?
5. How many times a day should we brush our teeth?
6. How long should we spend brushing our teeth?
7. How long does the writer spend cleaning his teeth?
8. How does the writer go to work?
9. Where does he work?
10. What does he do on his way to work?

At the dentist

1. How often do you go to the dentist?
2. Do you like going to the dentist?
3. Are dentists included in the National Health Insurance?
4. Are fillings included in the National Health Insurance?
5. Have you ever had a tooth pulled out?
6. Have you ever had a tooth filled?
7. Did you have any kind of anaesthetic?
8. Describe what the dentist did to give you the anaesthetic.
9. Was the injection painful?
10. How long was it until the area was numbed?
11. Did you feel any pain after that?
12. Describe how a tooth is filled.
13. Describe how a tooth is pulled out.
14. What do they put in your mouth to control the saliva?
15. Can you speak when the dentist is working in your mouth?
16. What do you do when the dentist talks to you?
17. Have you ever had a filling without anaesthetic?
18. Which is better, a metal or paste filling?
19. What's a 'bridge'?
20. Do you know anybody who has one?
21. Do you know anybody who has false teeth?
22. How do they clean false teeth?
23. Can they bite something hard with their false teeth?
24. What are the disadvantages of having false teeth?
25. What are the advantages?
26. Are false teeth paid for by the N.H.S.?
27. How much are they in your country?
28. Have you ever had your teeth cleaned? How do they do it?
29. Do you look after your teeth?
30. How do you clean them?
31. Have you ever cleaned them with a dental floss?
32. What do you think of the noise made by the drill?
33. Do you think dentists should wear masks?
34. Why should they?
35. What is 'bad breath' due to?
36. What does tobacco do to teeth?
37. Why do some film stars have such white, regular teeth?
38. Which are stronger, white teeth or yellowish teeth?
39. Is toothpaste effective in cleaning teeth?
40. What do you do when you have no toothbrush?

28 · At the hairdresser's

Glossary
to mind
to comb
dyed
oily
crew cut
wig
braids
to wonder
to hate
laughing stock
set
sprung
mushrooms

Description of the scene:

Suggested roleplays and dialogues

- In a group of three, act out a conversation among the three women
- In pairs, act out a conversation between the man with the long hair and a hairdresser.
- In pairs, act out a conversation between two hairdressers about the man with long hair.

Make comments son the following statements:

- Some men go to have a manicure done at the hairdresser's
- Men shouldn't go to a women's hairdresser's.
- Some wives cut their husbands' hair.
- Men without hair are very attractive.
- Men prefer blondes.
- Perms are out of fashion.

Questions on the scene

- What are the three women doing?
- What do you think they are saying?
- What are they wearing?
- What's the man at the back doing?
- Why are they all looking at the young man?
- Where has he got his hands?
- What do you think the shop at the back is?

True or false. Give reasons

- African people have long wavy hair.
- Men with short hair are more manly.
- Men never dye their hair.
- Boys are more effeminate nowadays.
- Older men love going to a hairdresser's.

Questions based on language functions

- Where do people go for a haircut?
- How often do people have a haircut?
- What do you say to the hairdresser?
- What does a hairdresser do before cutting your hair?
- Do men usually have a shampoo?

Have you ever wondered why women love going to the hairdresser's, while men usually hate doing the same thing? Or at least, older men hate it, because we can't say the same thing about the new generation. When I was young, men would never dream of going to a women's hairdresser's; if somebody did, he would have been the laughing stock of his friends. Nowadays, however, more and more long haired boys like to have a shampoo and set in one of the mixed hairdresser's that have sprung like mushrooms all over the place.

Does that mean that nowadays boys are more effeminate than in other generations? Well, to be honest, the answer is, no. They are just the same as they have ever been. Habits change, fashions change, human nature remains the same.

Questions

1. Do women like going to the hairdresser's?
2. Do older men like it?
3. Were there mixed hairdresser's years ago?
4. What would happen if a man went to a women's hairdresser's?
5. Where do young boys have their hair cut nowadays?
6. Are there many mixed hairdresser's nowadays?
7. Are boys more effeminate nowadays?
8. Do habits change?
9. Do fashions change?
10. Does human nature change?

At the hairdresser's

1. Have you ever been to a hairdresser's?
2. Have you ever had a 'perm'?
3. Have you ever had a shampoo and set?
4. What's the difference between a barber's shop and a hairdresser's
5. Do you think men should go to the same hairdresser's as women?
6. Do you mind being there with people of the opposite sex?
7. What do you think, a hairdresser should be, a man or a woman?
8. Is it difficult to comb a woman's hair?
9. What's the present hair fashion in your country?
10. Which do you like, long hair or short hair for a girl?
11. Which do you like, long hair or short hair for a man?
12. What do you think of men with long hair?
13. What do you think of those pinnacle-like hair styles of your grandmother?
14. What are the advantages of having very long hair?
15. What are the disadvantages?
16. What do you think of those youngsters with hair dyed blue and made solid with lacquer?
17. Do you like men with greasy hair?
18. How often do you think men go to the hairdresser's?
19. Do you think that a woman can cut a man's hair?
20. Do you like men with a crew cut?
21. Do you like men like Yul Brinner?
22. Would you wear a wig if you were bald?
23. What does dye do to the hair?
24. Will you dye your hair when it goes white?
25. What colour hair do you like?
26. Do men prefer blondes really?
27. What colour hair do you prefer in the opposite sex?
28. What do you think of braids?
29. In what countries do women still wear braids?
30. Can you make a braid? How do you do it?
31. What sort of hair do African people have?
32. What is the advantage of having curly hair?
33. What's the disadvantage?
34. Do many women wear wigs? Why?
35. What is the advantage of a wig?
36. Have hair fashions changed much along the years?
37. How much do you pay in your country for a shampoo? a perm?
38. Do men go to the hairdresser's for a shampoo?
39. Can you have a manicure done at the hairdresser's?
40. Can you describe what they do to your hands?

29 · At the zoo

Glossary
To lock up
to breed
earth
slowest
cages
warden
seal
partner
to look forward
grim-looking
to gaze
peanuts
yawning
sloshing
mud
flapping
tracks
monkey
challenge

Description of the scene:

Suggested roleplays and dialogues

· In pairs, act out a conversation between the zoo keeper and a visitor.
· In pairs, act out a conversation between two children watching the monkeys.
· In a group, act out a conversation among several schoolchildren visiting the tigers and lions.

Make comments on the following statements:

· Animals should not be kept in captivity.
· Safari parks are dangerous.
· To be a warden in a zoo is dangerous.
· Animals do not breed in captivity.
· People are not allowed to feed animals in the zoo.

Questions on the scene

· Are these animals in a zoo?
· Where do you think they are?
· What are they called?
· What's coming along the path?
· What part of the world do you think it is?
· How many trees can you see?
· How many giraffes are there in the picture?

True or false. Give reasons

· Animals in captivity often refuse to eat.
· The lion is the fastest animal on earth.
· An aquarium is a sort of zoo for fish.
· Monkeys like peanuts.
· Lions hunt. Lionesses don't.
· Giraffes have long necks to reach the leaves of the trees.

Questions based on language functions

· What time of the year do people go to the zoo?
· What do tigers eat?
· Why do you think the giraffes are running?
· What do giraffes eat?
· Does it rain much in that country?

Who hasn't spent a day at the zoo as a child? When I was a child I used to look forward to my father's trip to London. While he met his business partners in a grim-looking office in the West-end, my mother used to take us to see the animals at London zoo.

Looking back on those happy days, I remember gazing open-mouthed at the agile monkeys always eating peanuts; the ever yawning hippos sloshing in the mud, or the trumpeting elephants flapping their ears challengingly.

It was fascinating to watch all the different animals: tigers, lions, leopards, panthers, crocodiles...

One could imagine facing these animals in their habitat; hunting lions in the savannas of Africa or following the tracks of a huge tiger in the jungles of India.

Questions

1. What did the writer do when he went to London?
2. What did his father do in London?
3. What animals did the writer gaze open-mouthed at?
4. What did the monkeys do all the time?
5. What did the hippos do?
6. What did the elephants do?
7. What other animals are mentioned
8. Where do lions live?
9. Where do tigers live?
10. What did the writer imagine himself doing?

At the zoo

1. Have you ever been to a zoo?
2. Have you got a zoo in your home town?
3. What sort of animals can you see in the zoo?
4. Which are your favourite animals?
5. Are all animals locked up behind bars?
6. How, do you think, animals should be kept?
7. Do animals breed in captivity?
8. Are wild animals dangerous when they are in captivity?
9. Are you allowed to feed animals at the zoo?
10. What do you give to the monkeys?
11. Which is the biggest animal in the zoo?
12. Which is the fastest animal on earth?
13. Which is the slowest?
14. Is an Aquarium the same as a zoo?
15. What's the difference?
16. What's a safari park?
17. Have you ever been to one?
18. Can you come out of the car in a safari park?
19. What sort of animals are there in a safari park?
20. What's the difference between a safari park and a zoo?
21. Can children ride an elephant in a safari park?
22. Are safari parks dangerous?
23. Can you have a picnic in a safari park?
24. Can you see monkeys roaming free in a safari park?
25. Why not? Do you think they would escape?
26. Would you like to be a warden in a zoo?
27. What jobs do you think they have to do?
28. Would you like to feed animals?
29. Would you like to clean the cages?
30. How would you clean a tiger's cage?
31. How would you feed a lion?
32. Do wardens get into the cages of these animals to clean them?
33. What sort of food do lions and tigers eat?
34. What about elephants, what do they eat?
35. What sort of food do monkeys eat?
36. What would you give a seal to eat?
37. What do you think giraffes eat?
38. What would you do if an animal refused to eat?
39. Why do you think an animal refuses food?
40. Can an animal be in love?

30 · On the beach

Glossary
tanned
scuba-diving
storm
to shake
lying
naked
burnt
roasted
toe
death
silly
way

Description of the scene:

Suggested roleplays and dialogues

· In pairs, act out a conversation between a life guard and an imprudent swimmer.
· In pairs, act out a conversation between a girl reading a book and a boy jumping over her, throwing sand all over her.
· In pairs, act out a conversation between the two joggers.
· In pairs, act out a conversation between a person who is drowning and a rescuer.

Make comments on the following statements:

· Transistor radios are annoying on the beach.
· Some people have private beaches.
· Many people like playing football on the beach.
· Some beaches have no life-guards.
· Scuba-diving is dangerous.
· Picnics should be allowed on the beach.

Questions on the scene

· How many people are there in the picture?
· How many of them are in the water?
· How many saling boats can you see?
· What are the two boys on the right side of the picture doing?
· What is the girl nearest to us going to do?
· Can you describe the boy sitting on the left?

True or false. Give reasons.

· The kiss of life can save a life.
· Arabas like to lie on the sand.
· The water on the coast is not polluted.
· All beaches have life-guards.
· Getting sun burnt is dangerous for health.

Questions based on language functions

· What does a boy say to ask his girlfriend if she wants to go jogging with him?
· What does she say to refuse?
· What does she say to her boyfriend to ask him to slow down a little?
· What does the boy say to her to make her run faster?
· How does he invite her to have something to drink when they finish jogging?

If one of our ancestors should rise from his tomb and look at one of our beaches in summer, he would probably shake his head with incredulity... and go back to the tomb.

What, on the earth, are these people doing lying in the sun half naked? He would wonder. These descendents of ours have gone mad. Why do they want to get burnt, roasted like chickens? Isn't it much nicer to the eye, and better for the health to keep your skin white? Even the Arabs in the desert, cover themselves from head to toe in order to protect their skin from the rays of the sun. Why do people nowadays try to burn themselves to death in such a silly way?

Questions

1. Would one of our ancestor be surprised if he saw our beaches?
2. What would he do?
3. What would he say to himself?
4. What would he think of the mental health of his descendents?
5. What do people do to themselves?
7. What do Arabs do?
8. Why?
9. Is it dangerous to get sun burnt?
10. What illness can an excess of sun produce?

On the beach

1. Have you ever been to the beach?
2. Do you live near a beach?
3. What are the advantages of living near one?
4. Are there any disadvantages?
5. Would you like to spend your holidays at the beach?
6. Which do you prefer, the mountains or the beach?
7. What's the difference?
8. Do you go to the beach to get sun tanned?
9. Do you take a book to the beach to read while you sun-bathe?
10. What do you think of people playing football on the beach?
11. What games can you play on the beach?
12. What other activities can you do on the beach?
13. Is the beach a good place to swim?
14. What's the difference between swimming in the sea and in a swimming-pool?
15. Are beaches dangerous?
16. Would you like to be a lifeguard on a beach?
17. What do lifeguards do?
18. What's the kiss of life?
19. Do you know how to do it?
20. Have you ever been surfing?
21. What do you think of it?
22. Is it dangerous?
23. What do you need to go surfing?
24. Can you go surfing without waves? Wind surfing, perhaps?
25. Do you have sandy beaches in your country?
26. Which beach would you like to go to if you were a millionaire?
27. What's the sea water like in your country?
28. Have you ever done any scuba-diving?
29. Have you done any underwater fishing?
30. What do you think of dogs on the beaches?
31. Should picnics be allowed on beaches?
32. What about transistor radios?
33. Would you like to have a private beach to yourself?
34. Are private beaches allowed in your country?
35. Do you ever go to the beach in winter?
36. What do you often find on the beach after a storm or tempest?
37. Is sea-water good for your health?
38. In which way is it good?, walking in it?, drinking it?
39. Is the water on the coast clean nowadays?
40. What is pollution due to?

31 · Tourism

Glossary
flowery
lazy
trekking
hitch-hiker
to cycle
leader
tempted
pattern
enrich
to give vent
to store

True or false. Give reasons.
- Most tourists go to visit monuments.
- Tourism is a good source of income for the country.
- Tourists walk about with three cameras hanging from their necks.
- Tourists carry a phrase book with them.
- Winter tourists go to skiing stations.

Description of the scene:

Suggested roleplays
- In pairs, act out a conversation between the tourist and the man being photographed.
- In pairs, act out a conversation between two tourists visiting Pisa.
- In groups, act out a conversation among several tourists in the hotel lounge.
- In pairs, act out a converstion between two 'natives' about a group of tourists.

Make comments on the following statements:
- Tourism brings a lot of money to the country.
- Most tourists go to the beaches.
- Trekking is for young people.
- Most tourists come from the north.
- Hitch-hiking is very cheap tourism.

Questions on the scene
- Which side is the Pisa Tower leaning to?
- What's the fat woman doing?
- What's the nationality of the tourist behind the fat woman?
- What's the fat woman wearing?
- What's the man nearest to us wearing?
- What has he got in his hand?
- What's his nationality?
- Are there more people in the picture?

Questions based on language functions
- How does the fat woman ask the 'native' if she wants to take a photo?
- What does the man say to refuse?
- What does the woman say to the man to ask him to smile?
- What does the other tourist say to the fat woman to make her hurry?
- How does the Japanese tourist ask the Italian to lift the flag and move a little to the left?
- How do you think the Italian tells the Japanese that it is forbidden to take photographs?

What is a tourist? Some will be tempted to answer that it is a strange creature wearing flowery patterned shirts, shorts and walking about with three cameras hanging from their necks. Others, specially the economists, will consider the tourists as 10% of the national income.

Most tourists come from the northern countries looking for the sunny beaches of the south. Others prefer to enrich their knowledge visiting museums and old castles. Then, there are the more energetic ones that take advantage of their summer holidays to give vent to the excess of energy they have stored during the winter: they go climbing, trekking or camel riding across the desert.

Questions

1. What is the description of a typical tourist?
2. What is a tourists to an economist?
3. What percentage of the country's economy is provided by tourism?
4. What do most tourists look for?
5. How do others enrich their knowledge?
6. What does a typical tourist wear round his neck?
8. Where do most tourists come from?
9. What do the more energetic tourists do?
10. Where do some people go riding camels?

Tourism

1. Have you ever been out of your country?
2. Did you consider yourself as a tourist then?
3. How would you define a tourist?
4. Do you think of a tourist as wearing shorts and a flowery shirt?
5. Do you have many tourists in your country?
6. What countries do they come from?
7. Which country receives the biggest number of tourists in the world?
8. How do tourists come to your country?
9. What part of your country do they usually go to?
10. Has your country many beaches, a long coastline?
11. Do you have any other kind of tourism?
12. Do you have any monuments or buildings to visit?
13. What country would you like to visit as a tourist?
14. What would you do in that country?
15. Are you a lazy tourist or an active one?
16. Define what a lazy tourist is.
17. What is your opinion of an active tourist?
18. What's trekking?
19. What activities would you suggest for an active tourist?
20. Has a tourist ever asked you for directions?
21. In which language did you answer him?
22. Did he understand you?
23. Did he have a pocket phrase book in his hand?
24. What did he/she ask you?
25. What does a tourist usually ask about?
26. What is a hitch-hiker?
27. Can such a person be considered as a tourist?
28. Have you ever been hitch-hiking?
29. What's your opinion of it?
30. What do you think of people who cycle around the world?
31. Are they tourists?
32. Which countries are leaders in the tourist trade?
33. Would you like to work with tourists, as a receptionist for example?
34. Do you think tourists consider themselves superior to other people?
35. Which country 'provides' the greatest number of tourists?
36. Which means of transport are used by most tourists?
37. Were there many tourists last century?
38. When did the tourist boom start?
39. Has wealth anything to do with tourism?
40. Would you like to go on a package holiday or on your own?

32 · Being a king

Glossary
yacht
commoner
inherit
priority
throne
subjects
dream
to reign
to rule
role

Description of the scene:

Questions on the scene
- Where's the old king sitting?
- Is he a modern king?
- Can you describe the expression on his face?
- What's he wearing?
- What does his attitude suggest?
- What has he got on his head?

True or false. Give reasons.
- Kings have a lot of power nowadays.
- In Egypt there never were kings.
- Kings vote in the elections.
- Anybody can become a king.
- All countries have kings.
- In the old days, in China the ruler was the mandarin.

Suggested roleplays
- In pairs, act out a conversation between the king and newspaper reporter.
- In pairs, act out a conversation between the king and the queen about the country's political situation.
- In pairs, act out a conversation between Henry VIII and one of his many wives before being beheaded.

Make comments on the following statement:
- A modern king is very different from a king in the Middle Ages.
- Republicans don't believe in kings and queens.
- Monarchy is good for the country.
- Kings and queens can't walk about the streets alone.
- A Prince should study foreign languages.

Questions based on language functions
- What does a prince say to ask his father for advice about the day he becomes a king?
- What does the king say to refuse his son marrying a commoner?
- What does the queen say to her daughter to ask her not to go out at nights to the discotheques?

One of the typical subjects for a school composition is «If I were a king». Who hasn't dreamt of being a king? What boy hasn't closed his eyes and let his imagination run wild seeing himself as a powerful king whose smallest wishes are orders to a thousand servants.

Modern kings and queens are, however, very different from the idea we have of a powerful king like Henry VIII, for example.

Democracy has brought a modern conception of the monarchy in which the king reigns but doesn't rule. The role of a modern king is limited to be the visible head of the country, but the real rulers are the politicians; men and women elected by the people.

Questions

1. What's the typical subject for a school composition?
2. What do boys often do?
3. How many servants does the writer mention?
4. Are modern kings similar to Henry VIII?
5. Do you know what Henry VIII is famous for?
6. What is modern conception of the monarchy?
7. What is the role of a modern king?
8. Who are the real rulers of a democratic country?
9. Who elects the political party that governs the country?
10. Is your country a democracy? Do you have a king?

Being a king

1. Would you like to be a king?
2. Do you think it's easy being a king?
3. What activities does a king do?
4. Is it pleasant to see famous personalities?
5. Should a king speak foreign languages?
6. Do you have a king in your country?
7. Do people like him?
8. What do you think of monarchy in general?
9. Should there be kings in a modern country?
10. Do kings have political power in the European countries?
11. Did kings have a lot of power in the old days?
12. What's better?
13. Should a prince go to university?
14. What career should a prince study to prepare himself to become a king?
15. Should a prince study in foreign countries?
16. Which countries do you think he should study in?
17. Should a king receive money from the country's treasury?
18. Do kings usually have a lot of private money?
19. Do kings have holidays?
20. Where do they usually spend their holidays?
21. What sort of holidays do they have?
22. Can you think of any king or queen that has a big yacht?
23. If a man marries a queen, does he become king?
24. What's the difference between a king and an emperor?
25. Do you know of any king or queen who abdicated from the throne because of his/her love of a commoner?
26. Can you think of any disadvantages of being a king?
27. Do kings have private lives?
28. Have you ever seen a king walking along the street alone?
29. Do you think that is possible? Why not?
30. Are kings allowed to vote in the political elections?
31. Why not?
32. Are there more monarchies now than in the old days?
33. What's it due to?
34. In the ancient Rome, Egypt, China or Persia they didn't have kings, what did they have?
35. How many countries have kings or queens nowadays?
36. Do you know who the first king was in your country?
37. Are kings elected by the people the same as the presidents?
38. Who succeeds to the throne when the king dies?
39. Has a prince priority over a princess to the throne?
40. Do you agree with that?

33 · Politics

Glossary
full-time job
evils
agree
fulfilled
kind of
cradle
to force
campaign

Description of the scene:

True or false. Give reasons
- In most democratic countries elections take place every four or five years.
- What the candidates promise is always fulfilled.
- Dictatorship is better than democracy.
- Candidates never promise to reduce taxes.
- A monarchical country is never democratic.
- A king reigns but doesn't rule.

Suggested roleplays
- In pairs, act out a conversation between a union leader and the president of the Goverment.
- In pairs, act out a conversation between the two leaders of the main political parties.
- In pairs, act out a conversation between a candidate for president and a voter who is undecided.

Make comments on the following statements:
- Democracy admits the existence of different ideologies.
- Dictatorship is good for the country.
- Greece was the cradle of democracy.
- Kings should rule the country.

Questions on the scene
- What are these two people doing? Can you describe the face of the man on the right?
- To which party do you think he belongs?
- Do you think the man on the left belongs to the socialist party?
- What's the man on the right wearing?
- What's the man on the left wearing?
- Where has he got his hands?
- What's taking place?

Questions based on language functions
- What does a socialist leader say to ask the conservative leader if he wants to discuss the pensions?
- What does the conservative leader say to refuse the socialist leader's invitation?
- How does the conservative leader invite the socialist leader to have lunch with him and discuss politics?
- How do you think somebody tells people that it is forbidden to discuss politics in a certain place?

Have you ever heard a politician speaking in an election campaign? Have you ever wondered at the incredible amount of things that they promise to do?

It's curious, but all candidates promise more or less the same things; they will all build more roads, hospitals, schools; they will reduce taxes and inflation, force the prices down and increase the pensions. However, when they come to power most of the promises they had made during the election campaign come to nothing.

There's little money left for roads; schools and hospitals will have to wait for better times; taxes can't be reduced because there's a deficit, and inflation is impossible to control due to the increase of the price of oil in the Arab countries...

Questions

1. What's the first question the writer asks you?
2. Do politicians promise many things?
3. Do candidates promise different things?
4. What do they say about hospitals and schools?
5. What will they reduce?
6. What will they do with pensions?
7. What happens to all the promises of the election campaign?
8. Is there a lot of money for roads, etc?
9. Why can't taxes be reduced?
10. Why can't inflation be controlled?

Politics

1. Do you like politics? Why not?
2. Do you ever discuss politics with your friends?
3. What do you think of politicians? Are they honest?
4. Are there many political parties in your country?
5. Mention the most important ones.
6. Which party won the last elections?
7. How many years have they been in power?
8. How often do you have general elections in your country?
9. Do you think a president should be in power more than two legislation periods?
10. Should politics be a full-time job?
11. What do you think of democracy?
12. What is democracy?
13. Can you have democracy without political parties?
14. What are the advantages of democracy?
15. What are the disadvantages?
16. What does a politician do? What's his job?
17. What are the main political parties in G.B.?
18. Which one is in power now?
19. What are the main political parties in the USA?
20. Which one is in power now?
21. Do you think politicians get too much or too little money?
22. Would you like to be a politician? Why?
23. It is said that democracy is the least of evils, do you agree?
24. What is another alternative to democracy?
25. Do you know of countries that have no democracy?
26. Would you like to live in one of those countries?
27. Is democracy good or bad for the country in general? Why?
28. What does 'liberty of expression' mean to you?
29. What do you think the limits are to this 'liberty'?
30. Do you vote in the elections?
31. What's the difference between a 'general election' and a local election'?
32. When you vote, do you vote for the party or for the person?
33. What do you think of election campaigns?
34. How do parties get money for that? Who pays for it?
35. Should candidates confront each other on TV in discussions?
36. In our present world of TV, are campaigns necessary?
37. Do you think the party in power has fulfilled its promises?
38. What would be the best kind of government?
39. Should candidates explain their programmes?
40. Which country is the cradle of democracy?

34 · Religions

Glossary
humankind
rites
outstanding
priest
priestess
newly
punishment
houri
witch
veil

Description of the scene:

Suggested roleplays

- In pairs, act out a conversation between a catholic and a Moslem trying to convert each other.
- In pairs, act out a conversation between a protestant and a catholic giving their points of view about their religions.
- In pairs, act out a conversation about an 'inquisitor' and a woman accused of being a witch.

Make comments on the following statements:

- Catholic priests can't get married.
- All religions are similar.
- Muslim women have to wear a veil.
- Jews are still waiting for the Messiah
- Some religions believe in reincarnation.
- There are priestesses in some religions.

Questions on the scene

- What's the man on the left holding in his right hand?
- What's the man sitting holding in his hand?
- What are they?
- Do you know of what order?
- What are they both wearing?
- What's the expression of the accused man?
- What's he wearing?
- What's the man on the right?
- What's he holding in his hand?

True or false. Give reasons

- Witches were burnt at the stake.
- Catholic religion has changed a lot lately.
- Protestant priests are married.
- All muslims have to go to Mecca once in a lifetime.
- Jesus ordered his disciples to build large churches.
- All christians believe in the virginity of Mary.

Questions based on language functions

- What does the Dominican on the left say to ask the accused if he has anything to say?
- What does the accused say to deny the accusation?
- What does the Dominican sitting say to ask the accused to sign the document?
- How does the Dominican invite the accused to repent of his sins?

Some people wonder why there are so many religions in the world. How is it possible that people adore so many different Gods? Could it be possible that one religion is right while all the others are wrong? Who is in possession of the truth? Are there such things as heaven and hell? If there are, what are they like?

Christians believe in eternal punishment while Budists are certain that our destiny is our union with God after several lives. Is reincarnation a fact? Do we reincarnate? If so, When? Why?

Moslems believe that they'll go to Paradise with 60 beautiful houris if they die bravely in battle. I'm trying to find out if women who die bravely in battle will also go to the same Paradise surrounded by 60 attractive young men.

Questions

1. What do some people wonder?
2. Do people adore the same God?
3. Is one religion right while the others are wrong?
4. What does the writer say about heaven?
5. What do Christians believe?
6. What do Buddhists believe?
7. What does the writer say about reincarnation?
8. What do Moslems believe?
10. What is a houri?

Religions

1. Are you religious?
2. What do you think of religion in general?
3. How many religions do you know?
4. What are the differences between them?
5. Do you think religion is necessary to humankind?
6. What is the attitude of young people towards religion?
7. What's the predominant religion in your country?
8. What do you think of religious 'rites'?
9. What do you call a person who doesn't believe in God?
10. Do you think a person is better if he/she is religious?
11. What is the most outstanding service in your religion?
12. Do you have priests in your religion?
13. Can women be priestesses in your religion?
14. Do you think women are neglected in that sense?
15. Do people have to attend a certain service in your religion?
16. How often do they have to meet?
17. Is modern man more or less religious than in the past?
18. Is religion more or less necessary than in the old days?
19. In what sense has religion changed in the last centuries?
20. What do you know about Islam?
21. Who was their Prophet?
22. What sort of paradise awaits a Moslem?
23. Where does a muslim have to go once in his life time?
24. What do religions usually teach people?
25. What do you know about Buddhism?
26. Do you believe in reincarnation?
27. How do Buddhists find a newly born Lama?
28. Do you think the Lama is reincarnated?
29. What do you know about the 'Inquisition'?
30. Can you think of any wars fought in the name of religion?
31. Do you think it is legitimate to kill in the name of God?
32. What is heresy?
33. Should it be condemned?
34. Who started the Christian religion?
35. What was the only commandment of Jesus?
36. Do you think men have followed his commandments?
37. Why are there so many differences between Christians?
38. What do you know about the Jews?
39. Who was the most important Prophet for them?
40. Was Jesus the Messiah for them or are they still waiting for him?

35 · Popular festivals

Glossary

pilgrimage
hermit
bull
disguise
float parade
entertainments
world-wide
stabbed
alley
gored

Description of the scene:

Suggested roleplays

- In pairs, act out a conversation between two boys running in front of the bulls.
- In pairs, act out a conversation between two of the bulls.
- In a group, act out a conversation among several people at the end of the festivals.
- In pairs, act out a conversation among two tourists in the carnivals in Rio.

Make comments on the following statements:

- The carnivals of Rio are dangerous.
- Christmas is a Christian celebration.
- Women do not run in front of the bulls.

- The 12th October is the celebration of the discovery of America.
- The 'Sanfermines' is the best known festival all over the world.

Questions on the scene

- How many bulls are there in the picture?
- How many people are running in front of the bulls?
- How many people can you see on the balconies?
- Are the houses new?
- What's the matter with the man running in the last position?
- What's the man on the balcony pointing at?
- What are the people running wearing?

True or false. Give reasons

- Several people die every year in the 'Sanfermines'.
- The life of a bull that gores someone is spared.
- In Rio the carnivals are held during the summer.
- Many people are murdered during the carnivals.
- Wine is given out free during the 'Sanfermines'.
- A big festival takes place in America on the 4th July to celebrate the discovery of the Continent.

Questions based on language functions

- What does a girl say to ask for permission if she wants to run in front of the bulls?
- What does the man in charge say to refuse the girl's petition?
- What does one of the runners say to another to ask him not to push?
- How does one of the runners invite another to have something to drink when they finish running?
- How do you think the man in charge tells the girl that women can't run in front of the bulls?

In some countries popular festivals have reached world-wide fame. Some of the most well known are the Carnivals in Rio, the Chinese New Year in Taiwan, or the San Fermin in Pamplona.

In all of them thousands of tourists come from all over the world to immerse themselves in a sea of wild music and dancing in order to forget their daily problems for a week.

It doesn't matter if tourists are stabbed in an alley of Rio, or gored to death by a bull in Pamplona. It all adds to the attraction of the festivals.

Questions

1. What have reached world-wide fame?
2. What is Rio de Janeiro famous for?
3. What do the Chinese celebrate?
4. What is Pamplona famous for?
5. Where do tourists come from?
6. What do they do during the festival?
7. Why do they dance wildly?
8. What happens sometimes in Rio?
9. What happens sometimes in Pamplona?
10. Does that dissuade people from going to those places?

Popular festivals

1. What is a popular festival?
2. Do you have festivals in your country?
3. What do people do during these festivals?
4. What sort of entertainment is there?
5. Are they religious festivals?
6. What are the most famous ones in your country?
7. Do people drink?
8. How many days do they usually last?
9. Do you wear special clothes in these festivals?
10. Are there any processions?
11. Do you have a pilgrimage to a hermitage, for example?
12. Have you heard of 'San Fermines' in Spain?
13. Are they famous?
14. How long do they last?
15. What's the main attraction of 'San Fermines'?
16. Is it dangerous to run in front of a bull?
17. Would you do it?
18. Where do many people sleep during the night?
19. Do you have anything like that in your home town?
20. Do you have carnivals in your country?
21. Do people disguise themselves?
22. Do you have a float parade?
23. Is a carnival of religious origin?
24. What about Christmas? Do you celebrate it in your country?
25. Is Christmas a religious celebration? What religion?
26. What is celebrated?
27. What do people give at Christmas?
28. Mention some more famous festivals. Where are they located?
29. Do you think young people like festivals?
30. Why do you think that is?
31. Are festivals expensive?
32. How much do you spend in a three-day festival?
33. What do you spend the money on?
34. Do you think you can enjoy yourself without spending money?
35. Have you heard of the Munich beer festival?
36. What do they celebrate there?
37. What do they eat and drink?
38. What do people celebrate on the 12th of October in many countries?
39. What do they celebrate in America on the 4th of July?
40. Look at the calendar and mention all the festivals and celebrations you can think of.

36 · Party time

Glossary
records
loud
New Year's eve
to enjoy
to be worth
jealous
to chat
to spread
warehouse
allow
wedding
approach

Description of the scene:

Suggested roleplays

- In pairs, act out a conversation between a boy and a girl dancing that meet for the first time.
- In pairs, act out a conversation between a boy and a girl. He asks her for a dance.
- In pairs, act out a conversation between two people who sit tired after having danced for a long time.
- In a group, act out a conversation among several people discussing the type of music they want to put on.

Make comments on the following statements:

- Children have parties at Christmas time.
- Parties are very noisy.
- Parties help boys and girls to meet.
- Young people shouldn't drink spirits at parties.
- Modern dancing is very tiring.
- Ballroom dancing is old fashioned.
- Parties help shy youngsters to meet.

Questions on the scene

- Are these people dancing in a garage?
- How many people are there? Can you describe them?
- How many people are sitting?
- How many of them wear glasses?
- Are the girls wearing skirts?
- What do you think the man sitting is drinking?
- What sort of music are they dancing to?

True or false. Give reasons

- Discotheques are quiet places.
- People can have a nice chat in a dicotheque.
- Parties help to bring young people together.
- New Year's eve parties go on all night.
- Young people go to dancing schools to learn to dance.
- Grown ups don't like pop music.

Questions based on language functions

- What does a boy say to ask a girl if she wants to go to a party?
- What does the girl say to refuse the invitation?
- What does the girl say to the boy to ask him when and where the party is going to take place?
- How does a boy invite a girl to have something to eat when they finish dancing?
- How do you think the barman tells them that they have nothing to eat?

Most people love parties. It's in human nature to want an opportunity to chat with other people over a glass of beer or while eating caviar sandwiches.

Party mania begins at an early age. Mothers are the ones that contribute to the spreading of it by organizing birthday parties for their young children. A five-year-old child spends his weekends going to the birthday parties of all his classmates. Later on in life they prefer to organize their own parties in the garage or the warehouse of one of their parents. Older people are not so inclined to go to these social meetings, but even so, most of us like to meet other people, even if it's only at the local church.

Questions

1. What do most people do?
2. What do people like if they have a chance?
3. When does party mania begin?
4. Who contributes to that?
5. What does a five-year-old child do at weekends?
6. Do their mothers organize their parties later in life?
7. Where do they have their parties?
8. Are older people as inclined as young people to go to parties?
9. What does the writer call the parties for older people?
10. Where do these people sometimes meet?

Party time

1. Have you ever been to a party?
2. What do you do at a party?
3. Do you play games? What sort of games?
4. Do you drink spirits? What else do you drink?
5. Do you listen to records or dance?
6. What sort of records do you listen to?
7. Do you dance tangos or waltzes?
8. Where do young people have parties?
9. When do they have them?
10. Until what time do parties go on?
11. Do you think parties should go on all night?
12. Do you have parties at Christmas?
13. What about New Year's Eve?
14. On what other occasions do you have parties?
15. Do you enjoy yourself at parties?
16. How do you feel the next day?
17. Is it worth it?
18. Isn't it better to have a party during the day?
19. Do you think you have a better chance of meeting boys/girls at parties?
20. What do you think of very loud music?
21. Do your parents like it? Why not?
22. What do your parents think of modern dancing?
23. What do you think of old style dancing?
24. Have you seen your parents dancing to pop music?
25. Did your parents go to parties in their youth?
26. At what time were they allowed to get back home?
27. What will you do when your own children grow up?
28. What do you wear at parties?
29. Is a party the same as a wedding?
30. What's the difference?
31. Do you like weddings? Why?
32. What do you eat at a party?
33. Do you think people should smoke at parties? Why?
34. Do you think spirits give shy people courage?
35. Do you know many shy boys/girls?
36. Would you approach the boy/girl you like openly?
37. Are you jealous when your favourite boy/girl dances with others at a party?
38. Would you go to a party if you knew that he/she wasn't there?
39. Do parties help in boy/girl relationships?
40. In which way does it help?

37 · A department store

Glossary
to steal
to be caught
selling
foreign
to join
kindness
friendliness
neatly
arranged
shelves
tempting
to pull
flashing
hovering
rockets
swords

- How many of them are climbing the stairs?
- How are they climbing?
- What are all these people wearing?
- What are they carrying?
- Is anybody wearing glasses?, and earrings?

True or false. Give reasons.

- The advantage of a department store is that you can find everything in there.
- Many things are stolen in a department store.
- Department stores never close.
- The restaurant floor is usually at the top.
- Department stores open on Sundays.
- In a department store you must pay cash.
- People suspected of stealing are searched at the exit.

Description of the scene:

Suggested roleplays

- In pairs, act out a conversation between a woman and the person at the information desk.
- In pairs, act out a conversation between a mother and a child that is climbing the escalator for the first time.
- In pairs, act out a conversation between a guard and a person caught stealing.
- In pairs, act out a conversation between a customer who wants to know where to pay and a cleaning woman.

Make comments on the following statements:

- Shopping in a department store is cheaper/more expensive.
- Children love department stores.
- Hidden cameras are watching you all the time.
- A lot of things are stolen.
- Little shops are disappearing because of supermarkets and department stores.

Questions on the scene

- How many people can you see all together?

Questions based on language functions

- What does a customer say to ask an employee where the toy section is?
- What does the employee say to tell the customer where the toy section is?
- What does a mother say to her child to be careful with the escalator?
- How does a male employee invite a female employee to eat when they finish working?
- How do you think the person in charge of the clothes department tells a little boy that he can't play hide and seek with his little brother?

I think they are fascinating! Department stores have always fascinated me. When I was a child my mother used to take me to London with her. She used to do her Christmas shopping at one of the big department stores in Oxford Street or Kensingon.

The escalators made me think I was in a fairy house. I never got tired of going up and down. Nevertheless, what really fascinated me most was the toy department. It was incredible the mountains of toys that were neatly arranged on the shelves, quietly tempting the open-eyed children that, like myself, were being pulled by their mothers by the hand. I was hypnotized by flashing police car lights, hovering helicopters, space rockets and shining swords.

Questions

1. What does the writer find fascinating?
2. Where did he go with his mother?
3. Where did she do her Christmas shopping?
4. What did the escalator make him think?
5. Did he get tired of going up and down?
6. What was it that fascinated him most?
7. Where there many toys?
8. What did the toys do to the children?
9. Did the mothers stay long in this section?
10. What was the writer hypnotized by?

A department store

1. Have you ever been to a department store?
2. Do you have many in your country?
3. And in your home town? Do you have any?
4. What can you buy in a department store?
5. What are the advantages of shopping there?
6. What are the disadvantages?
7. Do you like walking about in one?
8. Do people buy things that they didn't intend to buy?
9. What's the difference between a department store and a supermarket?
10. And a hypermarket?
11. Do you like escalators?
12. Is it more expensive shopping in department stores? why?
13. Do you think people steal in these places?
14. Is it difficult to steal things in department stores?
15. Have you ever seen a person being caught stealing?
16. How do guards approach these people?
17. What do they do with them?
18. How are things watched? Have you seen TV monitors?
19. Would you like to work in one of these places?
20. In which department would you like to work?
21. Is it the same working in a little shop as in a department store?
22. What is the difference in the selling technique?
23. Do you think sales people always tell the truth?
24. Can people change the things they've bought if they don't like them?
25. Do you think it's necessary to know foreign languages in this job?
26. Can you mention the different departments that there are in a big store?
27. Can you get something to eat or drink in a department store?
28. Where's the restaurant placed usually?
29. Is food expensive in these places?
30. What sort of service do you get? self-service? free buffet? served by waiters?
31. What time do these places open?
32. When do they close?
33. Do they close at dinner time?
34. Where do employees eat?
35. Do you think department stores should open on Sundays?
36. Is there competition between these stores and normal shops?
37. Is competition fair?
38. What's happening to many small shops?
39. What can small shops do to defend their interests? Can they join forces?
40. What do people appreciate in small shops? kindness?, friendliness?

38 · Studying or working

Glossary

to get paid
unemployed
dying
in order to
middle aged
seeking
moral
chances
greater

Description of the scene:

Suggested roleplays

· In pairs, act out a conversation between a student and a worker.
· In pairs, act out a conversation between the father and a son who doesn't want to study.
· In pairs, act out a conversation between a young man who is working and wants to study and the head of the night school.

Make comments on the following statements:

· Working is better because you get some money.
· Studying is better because you'll get qualifications for a better job.
· Working and studying is very hard.
· It impossible to get rich working.
· Housewives should get a salary.

Questions on the scene

· What does the dreaming girl do?
· What's her job?
· What's she dreaming of?
· What has she got in her left hand?
· What's there on her right?
· Who's the woman with the fur coat?
· What are the three people doing?

True or false. Give reasons

· Studying languages is important for a job.
· University students get paid for studying.
· Housewives get a good pay from the government.
· Bad students get grants.
· Working is possible to get lots of money.

Questions based on language functions

· What does the secretary say to her boss if she wants a pay rise?
· What does the boss say to refuse her demand?
· What does the secretary say to her boyfriend to tell him that they can't get married yet?
· What does the boss say to the secretary to make her work more hours?
· How does the boss invite the secretary for lunch?
· How do you think the secretary refuses the invitation?

When young people are studying they are dying for a job. They want to get some money in their hands, so very often they leave their studies in order to get a job.

Later in life, they are sorry they gave up their studies and wish they had continued getting some knowledge that would probably increase their chances of promotion or getting a better job.

As the head of a private technical school I often find that middle aged people come to our Centre seeking a qualification that they couldn't or did not want to get when they were younger.

The moral is: study while you can. The more qualifications you have, the greater your chances are of getting a good job.

Questions

1. What do young people want when they are studying?
2. Why do they want to get a job?
3. What happens later on in life?
4. What do they wish?
5. Does knowledge increase the chances of getting a better job?
6. What does the writer do? What's his job?
7. What does he find?
8. Why didn't these people have a qualification?
9. What's the moral of this essay?
10. What should you do if you want a good job?

Studying or working

1. Are you studying or working?
2. How many years do you have left to study?
3. What is better, to study or to work?
4. What are the advantages of studying?
5. What are the disadvantages?
6. What are the advantages of working?
7. What are the disadvantages?
8. What do people study for?
9. What do people work for?
10. Would you work if you didn't have to?
11. Do you think work is a bad thing?
12. Do you think some people can enjoy working?
13. What kind of people? What kind of work?
14. Do people enjoy studying?
15. Do you consider yourself a good student or a bad one?
16. Do you think studying languages is important for a job?
17. Should students get paid for studying?
18. Many people work and don't get paid, who are those people?
19. Should housewives get paid?
20. Are there many people working and studying?
21. How can they do it?
22. Do you know of any?
23. If they work when do they study?
24. Do you admire them? Why?
25. Do you have facilities to do that in your country?
26. Why do people work and study?
27. Does the government help these people in your country?
28. Are there many people unemployed with qualifications in your country?
29. Do you think it's worth studying nowadays?
30. Can you make a lot of money by working?
31. Can you make more money if you have qualifications?
32. Do people study because they want money?
33. Is getting rich your ambition in life?
34. What other ambitions do you have?
35. Do you think a housewife should work outside the home?
36. Is there a lot of unemployment in your country? What percentage?
37. Would you like to be your own boss?
38. Do you think it's easy to be your own boss?
39. Do you know any young people working for themselves?
40. How many hours do they work?

39 · Having a baby

Glossary

painful
to feed
to give the bottle
birth rate
pregnant
pregnancy
nursery
breast-fed
moaning
wheel chair
midwife
presently
to nod
so few

Description of the scene:

Suggested roleplays

- In pairs, act out a conversation between the woman in the picture and a friend.
- In pairs, act out a conversation between two boys who are talking about the woman in the picture.
- In pairs, act out a conversation between two girls about a pregnant woman.

Make comments on the following statements:

- Giving birth is very painful.
- Men should give birth.
- The period of pregnancy is very hard.
- Mothers should give birth at home.
- A baby should be breast-fed.
- Mothers to be should not smoke.

Questions on the scene

- Where's the woman sitting or lying?
- Where's the easy chair?
- What's she doing?
- What's the matter with her?
- What's the weather like?
- Can you describe the expression on her face?
- In which month of pregnancy is she?

True or false. Give reasons

- Pregnancy takes nine months.
- Breast-fed babies are healthier.
- Music is good for unborn babies.
- The birth rate is very low in developed countries.
- The emotional state of the mother affects the baby's temperament.
- Babies that are born feet first live shorter lives.

Questions based on language functions

- What does a pregnant woman say to her husband if she thinks the moment has arrived?
- What does the husband say if he can't find the keys of the car?
- What does the pregnant woman say to her husband to ask him to slow down a bit?
- What does she say to him to make him drive faster?
- How does the husband tell the nurses that the baby is about to be born?

My wife was going to have a baby! We rushed to hospital. I had never felt so nervous in all my life. I kept looking apprehensively at my wife moaning quietly in the passenger seat. I wouldn't like to have a son in the middle of the High Street.

At last we reached Mothers' Hospital and Janet was placed in a wheel chair. The midwife took her into a room and came out presently informing me that the baby was already on the way. She asked me if I wanted to be there at the time of birth. I nodded silently. Of course I wanted to see my son come into the world. I was just in time. by the time I had put on the green sterilized gown and rushed into the room, the baby was pushing his body outside. Soon a loud cry showed that he was very much alive. It was my son!

Questions

1. What was the matter with the writer's wife?
2. Where did they go?
3. How was the writer feeling?
4. Who took his wife to hospital?
5. What was the writer afraid of?
6. How was Janet taken into the hosptial?
7. What did the midwife say to the writer?
8. Did the writer want to be with his wife at the time of birth?
9. What did he have to put on?
10. What did the writer soon hear?

Having a baby

1. Have you ever had a baby?
2. Do you have a sister who has?
3. Do you think it's painful?
4. Should men have babies too?
5. What do you think of maternity? Is it nice, gratifying?
6. Should mothers feed the babies themselves or give them the bottle?
7. How many children should a family have?
8. Should mothers go to hospital to have a baby?
9. Would you like to have a baby at home?
10. What's the difference?
11. What happened in the old days?
12. How do Indians, Eskimos, etc., give birth?
13. What is a Caesarean operation?
14. What is the umbilical cord?
15. Is it dangerous for a baby to come out feet first?
16. What should the doctor do in that case?
17. What's the position of the foetus?
18. Do you think the foetus can feel or hear things?
19. Can the food eaten by the mother affect the baby?
20. What about the drinks, tobacco or drugs taken by the mother, do they affect the baby?
21. They say that the emotional state of the mother during pregnancy affects the future temperament of the baby, what do you think?
22. Is it expensive having a baby?
23. Should the government help?
24. What's the birth rate in your country?
25. Why do people have so few babies nowadays?
26. What do you think of the pregnancy period?
27. Should women go to the gym when they are pregnant?
28. What exercises are they recommended to do? What for?
29. Should parents go to pre-natal classes?
30. What are they taught in these classes?
31. Do you think a baby alters the daily life of a couple?
32. In which way is it different now?
33. Should a baby be fed during the night?
34. A baby cries very often, what do you think are the likely causes?
35. Should women stop working when they have a baby?
36. How long are they allowed to be off work?
37. Should babies be sent to nurseries?
38. What are the advantages of babies being brought up in nurseries?
39. What are the disadvantages?
40. Should babies be breast-fed?

40 · Cruising

Glossary
cruise
liner
likely
crew
to mix
to entertain
honeymoon
silver
wedding
troubles
seasick
huge
decks
to amuse

Description of the scene:

True or false. Give reasons

- A cruise ship is like a floating city.
- Two people often fall in love on those cruises.
- The crew mixes with the passengers.
- Cruise ships stop at many ports.
- A Mediterranean cruise is very typical.

Suggested roleplays

- In pairs, act out a conversation between a passenger and one of the employees explaining the activities in the ship.
- In threes, a conversation between the captain and a couple on their honeymoon.
- In pairs, act out a conversation between a seasick woman and a waiter.

Make comments on the following statements:

- A cruise is a relaxing holiday.
- Entertaining passengers is a pleasant job.
- Many people get seasick on those voyages.
- A liner is similar to a cruise ship.
- Cruises are expensive.
- Only older/elderly people go on cruises.

Questions on the scene

- What sort of ship is in the picture?
- How many life boats can you see?
- What's in the background of the picture?
- Can you see anybody on board?
- How many cabins do you think the ship has?

Questions based on language functions

- What does a passenger say if he wants to ask a beautiful waitress to have dinner with him?
- What does the waitress say to refuse the invitation?
- What does the man say to the waitresses to ask her to meet him that evening on deck?
- How does the waitress tell the man that they can't accept invitations from passengers?
- How does the man invite the waitress to meet him when they finish the voyage?

The ship was huge. It was like a floating city. I would never have imagined that there could be so many things in a ship. There were five decks. The two thousand passengers could enjoy things like: mini-golf, squash, tennis and volley ball; there was a gym, a running track, four swimming pools, a library, five cinemas, a music band, three dining halls, a bingo hall, ten pubs and six discotheques.

Plays, games and different activities were organized by special people to amuse the passengers. Children were paid special attention so that they wouldn't keep pestering their parents. A nursery looked after little children most of the day. It was the nearest thing to paradise that man could organize.

Questions

1. What was the ship like?
2. What does the writer say about it?
3. How many decks were there?
4. What games could they play?
5. How many swimming pools were there?
6. How many pubs were there?
7. What did special people organize?
8. Why were children paid special attention?
9. Was there anything for little children?
10. What is the opinion of the writer about the cruise?

Cruising

1. Have you ever been on a cruise?
2. What seas or places do cruises go to?
3. What are the ships used for cruising like?
4. What is life like on one of these ships?
5. What activities do people do on them?
6. What's the difference between a liner and a cruise ship?
7. Do you think children would like going on a cruise?
8. Do you have activities and games on a liner?
9. Are there different classes of passengers on a cruise ship?
10. Can you mention ports cruise ships are likely to visit?
11. Do they stay in these ports very long?
12. The captain must be a special type of person, why?
13. What do you think are the captain's jobs?
14. Does the captain have to be sociable?
15. Will there be dinner dances?
16. Do you have to pay at the restaurant?
17. What about the bar?
18. Can the crew mix with the passengers?
19. Do you think there are many romances on the 'love boats'?
20. Do lonely people go on a cruise alone?
21. Do you think a cruise is a relaxing holiday?
22. Is a cruise expensive? How much will it cost?
23. Would you like to work on a cruise ship?
24. What sort of job would you like to do?
25. Would you like to be the person who entertains the passengers?
26. What sort of entertainments would you prepare for them?
27. Would you like to be the captain of a cruise ship?
28. What sort of social problems does the captain have to face?
29. Do you find a lot of young people on a cruise?
30. What sort of passengers are likely to go on a cruise?
31. Would you go on a cruise on your honeymoon?
32. Would you go on a cruise on your silver wedding anniversary?
33. Is there a doctor on board one of these ships?
34. Can you think of troubles that the passengers may have?
35. Do people get seasick on those ships?
36. Have you ever felt seasick?
37. What can you do about it?
38. Do you feel like eating?
39. Could it happen that some people will spend part of their holidays in bed?
40. Will the shipping company refund the money?

41 · A desert Island

Glossary
cave
cast away
to be afraid
weapon
matches
to fish
to hunt
raw
raft
wild
lit
worn out
bare footed
shellfish
plentiful
goat
stock

Description of the scene:

Suggested roleplays
· In pairs, act out a conversation between two castaways the first day on the island.
· In pairs, act out a conversation between the two castaways the day they see a ship passing near the island.
· In a group of three, act out a conversation between the captain of the rescuing ship and the two castaways.

Make comments on the following statements:
· Many people would like to live on a desert island.
· Alone or with somebody else?
· With another person of the same sex or different sex?
· To live on an island for a year would be nice.
· Robinson Crusoe was happy on his desert island.

Questions on the scene
· What's this man doing?
· Has he been on this island very long?
· Can you describe the expression on his face?
· Is the island big?
· Where is he sitting?
· Is there anybody else with him?
· Can you see any animals or birds?

True or false
· Robinson Crusoe was written by Daniel Defoe.
· Robinson Crusoe spent many years living alone.
· Castaways are always very happy.
· To make a fire without matches is easy.
· To survive you would have to learn to fish and hunt.

Questions based on language functions
· What does a castaway say to the other if he wants to explore the island?
· What does the second castaway say if he doesn't want to go?
· What does the first castaway say to the second to ask him to collect some shellfish?
· What does the second castaway say to the first to help him collect shellfish?
· How do you think one of them will say to the other that they have to make a fire with two sticks?

Ever since Daniel Defoe wrote Robinson Crusoe, people have dreamt of living on a desert island.

This island, of course, would have to be located in the Pacific Ocean surrounded by clear, warm water where fish and shellfish would be plentiful. On the island there should be a lot of animals like sheep and goats and of course, fruit trees. The variety of them should be as wide as possible. A good dry cave should be at hand in case of storms; otherwise, the castaway would live in a wooden house by the beach. Ideally he should have his faithful dog with him and a good stock of books.

Questions

1. Who wrote Robinson Crusoe?
2. What have people dreamt of since then?
3. Where should the island be located?
4. What should the water be like?
5. What does the writer say about fish and shellfish?
6. What kind of animals should there be on the island?
7. What does he say about fruit trees?
8. Why does the writer want a dry cave?
9. Where would the castaway like to live?
10. What two things would a castaway like to have?

A desert Island

1. Have you ever been on a deserted island?
2. Would you like to be on one?
3. Would you like to be alone or with somebody?
4. Whom would you like to be with?
5. What things would you like to have with you?
6. How long would you like to be there?
7. Would you like to live on one?
8. What books would you like to have with you?
9. Do you think someone can be happy living alone?
10. Would you like to build your own house?
11. Would you prefer to live in a cave, perhaps?
12. Would you take animals to live with you?
13. What sort of animals?
14. What would you do first after being cast away on a desert island?
15. Would you be afraid? Of what?
16. How would you defend or protect yourself?
17. What weapons would you like to have?
18. Do you think you could build a house?
19. Would you be able to make a fire without matches?
20. What sort of food would you eat?
21. Would you fish? How?
22. Would you hunt? How?
23. How would you cook the food?
24. Would you eat raw meat or fish if you had to?
25. Would you try to make a raft or a boat?
26. If you had a boat would you leave the island?
27. What would you do attract the attention of passing ships?
28. Where would you like to live, on the coast or in the centre of the island?
29. Would you make sure there were no other human beings on the island? Why?
30. What would you do if there were wild animals?
31. If you had no matches and you made a fire with a stick, would you keep it lit or let it go out?
32. Would you keep your shoes on until they were worn out or would you walk bare footed?
33. Would you keep a diary? What sort of things would you write in it?
34. Would you explore the island?
35. How would you like the island to be? Describe your ideal desert island.
36. In what part of the world would you like it to be?
37. If you were rescued, would you write a book about your experiences?
38. What do you think the hardest part of living on a desert island would be?
39. What would be the most pleasant part of it?
40. Do you think Robinson Crusoe really existed? Who wrote the book? (Daniel Defoe)

42 · Reading

Glossary
encouraged
forced
habit
fond of
busy
to go
through
illiterate
will power
succeed
success

Description of the scene:

Suggested roleplays
- In pairs, act out a conversation between the two boys.
- In threes, act out a conversation between the mother and the two boys.
- In pairs, act out a conversation between the father and the mother of the boys about reading comics and not doing their homework.

Make comments on the following statements:
- Reading is good, even if it's reading comics.
- Books are expensive.
- Good writers earn a lot of money.
- Reading 'girly magazines' is a waste of time.
- A book is the best present you can get.
- Most of the 'best-sellers' are American.

Questions on the scene
- What are the two boys doing?
- What are they reading?
- Can you describe the expression on their faces?
- What's the comic about?
- What are the boys wearing?

True or false. Give reasons
- Many people give books at Christmas.
- English is the most widely read language in the world.
- A book may change your life.
- People in general read very little.
- Reading doesn't help to learn a language.
- You don't need to buy books in order to read.

Questions based on language functions
- What does a boy say to his mother if he wants to buy a comic?
- What does the mother say to refuse to give him money?
- What does a boy say to his friend to ask him to lend him a comic?
- What does the other boy say to suggest changing comics?
- How do you think the teacher will tell the children that they can't read comics in class?

Child Psychologists believe that reading is one of the best habits that should be encouraged into children. Ninety percent of the things we learn during our lifetime come through books; therefore if we can't read, we don't learn.

It is during the first years of our childhood that we should start reading. Never is the time better spent by parents as it is when getting their children to read.

According to statistics, successful people come from all walks of life; rich, poor, with university background or illiterate. However, there are two things that most successful people have: one is a very strong will power to succeed and the other is the habit of reading. Without will power nobody will succeed, without the habit of reading nobody will get very far on the road to success.

Questions

1. What do Child Psychologists believe?
2. What percentage of the things we learn come through books?
3. What will happen if we don't read?
4. When should we start reading?
5. What should parents do?
6. Where do successful people come from?
7. What do successful people have in common?
8. Can people succeed without will power?
9. Can people succeed without reading?
10. Do you like reading?

Reading

1. Do you read much?
2. What sort of books do you read?
3. Do you enjoy reading?
4. Do many people read in your country?
5. Are books expensive?
6. Should children be encouraged to read?
7. Should they be forced to read?
8. Should they read comics?
9. Do you think that, if they read comics now, later they will read books?
10. What are the advantages of reading?
11. Is it good to get the reading habit?
12. Do you get pleasure when buying a new book?
13. Do you ask for books at Christmas?
14. Are there many good writers in your country?
15. Do you have any Nobel Prize winners in your country?
16. Do you read in English or in your own language?
17. Does reading help to learn a language?
18. At what time do you read?
19. How many hours a week do you read for pleasure?
20. Do you read the paper?
21. Do you read magazines? What sort of magazines?
22. Are you fond of 'girly magazines'?
23. Do you think people should read more?
24. Do you think that people don't read so much because they are busy watching television?
25. What would you do to encourage people to read?
26. What sort of books should people be encouraged to read?
27. What have you learnt lately by reading books?
28. Have you read a best seller in the last few weeks?
29. Do you remember what it was about?
30. Have you ever read a book several times because you liked it?
31. What is your favourite book?
32. What story would you like to write?
33. Do you like historical, modern or futuristic stories?
34. Do you ever think of the writer when you read a book?
35. Do you prefer men or women writers?
36. Do you take into consideration the efforts and sacrifices that a writer has to go through in order to write a book?
37. Who is the greatest writer of all times?
38. Have you read any of his books?
39. Are there any famous women writers?
40. Can you mention some of them?

43 · Professions

Glossary

steps
to become
to esteem
kind of
drawer
lawyer
guilty
judge
fair
skilled
unqualified
to be over
strike

Description of the scene:

Suggested roleplays

· In pairs, act out a conversation between a man with a profession looking for work and a employer.
· In pairs, act out a conversation between a lawyer and a man accused of a crime.
· In pairs, act out a conversation between a father and a son/young man choosing his career.

Make comments on the following statements:

· Students can't always choose the degree they would like to study.
· It is difficult to become rich in a profession.
· Opportunities are greater if you have a profession.
· 50% of the millionaires are professionals, the other 50% are not.
· There are more people studying at universities than ever before.

Questions on the scene

· What do you think that man does?
· What's he doing at this moment?
· What has he got in his hand?
· What's he wearing?
· What has he got on his ear?
· What do you think he's drawing?

True or false. Give reasons

· Doctors get millionaire's salaries.
· Students can study the career they like best.
· Most artists become rich.
· All politicians are dishonest.
· A lawyer will defend a criminal even if he knows he's guilty.
· Judges are always right.
· The job of a journalist is sometimes dangerous.

Questions based on language functions

· What does a student say to his/her father if he wants to study a degree?
· What does the father say to inform his son/daughter that he has no money?
· What does the father say to his son/daughter that the career s/he has chosen is not very good?
· What does the son/daughter say to his/her parents that he has to go to study to another town?

What do you do? What's your profession?

We are all asked that question many times during our lifetime. In a very professionalized world, nowadays everybody is expected to have a profession. It is extremely difficult to get a job if you are not skilled in something. The days in which factories provided work for unqualified workers are over. Robots take the post of those. These automatic machines never complain, never get tired and never go on strike.

Even street sweepers are being taken over by mechanical devices that sweep the pavement as they go along at 10 m.p.h. The men who drive them are qualified; their profession is: street-cleaning technicians.

Questions

1. What question are we often asked?
2. What is everybody expected to have?
3. What is difficult nowadays?
4. What is over?
5. What takes the post of unqualified workers?
6. What do robots never do?
7. What is taking over street sweeping?
8. How fast do these machines go?
9. Are the drivers of these machines qualified?
10. What is the title they have?

Professions

1. What would you like to be?
2. Are you taking any steps to become one?
3. What do you have to do to become what you'd like to be?
4. What are the most esteemed professions in your country?
5. Would you like to be a doctor?
6. Can you describe a doctor's day?
7. Do they all do the same thing?
8. Is it a hard life?
9. How much money can a doctor get in your country working in a hospital?
10. What about engineering? Would you like to be an engineer?
11. Are there many kinds of engineers?
12. What do they do? Give some examples of their jobs.
13. Can they become rich in your country?
14. Would you like to be an artist?
15. What kind of artist would you like to become?
16. Painter, sculptor, artist, cartoonist, designer any other jobs related with art?
17. Perhaps you would like to be a writer.
18. What do you think of writers? Do they work a lot? Is it hard to be a writer?
19. Have you ever tried to write something? What?
20. Is it difficult to describe things?
21. What about a conversation? Is it difficult to write one?
22. Would you like to be a journalist?
23. What do you think journalists do?
24. Can you describe the things they may have to do?
25. Is that job dangerous?
26. What do you think of politicians?
27. Is that a profession?
28. Can a politician earn a good living?
29. What do you need to be a politician?
30. Which political party would you like to represent?
31. Do you have a parliament in your country?
32. Are politicians honest?
33. Mention cases in which politicians were corrupt.
34. How would you like to become a lawyer?
35. Describe a lawyer's job.
36. Are there many kinds of lawyers?
37. Do you think lawyers are honest?
38. Should a lawyer defend a criminal knowing that he is guilty?
39. Would you like to be a judge?
40. Is it difficult to give a fair verdict?

44 · Actors

Glossary
a play
to earn your living
handsome
stage
Middle Ages
Easter
poverty
carts

Description of the scene:

Suggested roleplays

· In pairs, act out a conversation between two actors or actresses of a play or a serial you see on TV.
· In pairs, act out a conversation between a film star and a journalist interviewing him/her.
· In pairs, act out a conversation between a film director and a film star when they are going to shoot a scene.

Make comments on the following statements:

· Film stars get a lot of money.
· American actors are very good.
· Film stars get divorced very easily.
· There are training schools for actors and actresses.
· Old actors and actresses were better than today's
· Sexy films should be forbidden.
· In the Middle Ages actors and actresses were far from rich.

Questions on the scene

· How many people are there on the stage?
· What are they doing?
· What are they wearing?
· What has one of them got on her lap?
· Can you describe the position of both?
· What's there on the floor next to the woman?

True or false. Give reasons

· Actors and actresses have to repeat the same scene on films many times.
· In a play the scenes can be repeated.
· Acting in front of a camera is very impersonal.
· Most actors and actresses are divorced.
· Centuries ago actors and actresses were very poor.
· In the Middle Ages some plays were performed inside churches.

Questions based on language functions

· What does the film director say to an actor if he wants to repeat the scene?
· What does the actor say if he doesn't want to repeat it?
· What does the film director say to an actress if he wants her to put more life in the acting?
· How does the film director say to the actor that he has to swim across a river full of crocodiles?
· How does the film star say to everybody that they have to keep quiet, because they are shooting a scene?

Acting is one of the oldest professions in the world. Hundreds of years before Christ, the Greeks wrote and produced plays that are staged even today.

During the Middle Ages plays called «mystery plays» were performed in churches, specially during the Easter period and Christmas.

In those days, in fact, until very recently, most actors were amateurs; and the few that dedicated their lives to acting lived in extreme poverty. For hundreds of years, caravans of carts pulled by old tired horses, went from town to town. They put up a stage in the local stable and tried to make people laugh or cry for a penny each.

Questions

1. Is acting very old?
2. What did the ancient Greeks do?
3. When did they do it?
4. What happened in the Middle Ages?
5. What time of the year did they perform the «Mystery plays»?
6. Were actors professionals?
7. Were the professional actors rich?
8. How did actors live in the Middle Ages?
9. When did they act?
10. Was it expensive to see them?

Actors

1. Have you ever acted in a play?
2. Would you like to earn your living acting?
3. Has an actor an easy life?
4. What are the working hours of a film star?
5. Can they go home for lunch?
6. Are there good actors and actresses in your country?
7. Can you mention some?
8. Has any actor in your country ever won an Oscar?
9. Do actors get a lot of money in your country?
10. How do they compare with American actors?
11. Do you like American actors/actresses?
12. Are modern actors better or worse than the old ones?
13. Can you mention old 'glories' of the 50's or 60's?
14. Can you remember any actor/actress of the old silent films?
15. Mention actors/actresses that have won Oscars.
16. Mention some good modern actors.
17. Do you remember any films in which an actor has won an Oscar?
18. Do you think it's difficult to act?
19. How many times do actors have to repeat the scenes?
20. What do you think of sex scenes?
21. How far should they go?
22. Have sexy films influenced public morality?
23. Is there a lot of difference between acting in a theatre and in front of a camera?
24. What are the advantages and disadvantages of the theatre?
25. What are the advantages and disadvantages of films?
26. What about television? What do you think of live transmissions?
27. Why do they bring audiences to the studios?
28. Is it difficult to act in front of a camera with no audience?
29. Can you tell when someone is acting?
30. Do theatre actors get more or less money than film stars?
31. Do you think actors are intelligent? Do they have a good memory?
32. Are actors/actresses always handsome and beautiful?
33. Mention actors/actresses that are arrogant.
34. Mention places where actors live.
35. Do actors/actresses get divorced very often?
36. Mention some who are famous for the number of divorces they went through.
37. On the other hand some actors/actresses have been married for years. Do you know of any?
38. Do you think the life of an actor is appropriate for married life?
39. Are there training schools for actors/actresses in your country?
40. Do you think you can learn to act?

45 · Football

Glossary
referee
mistakes
fan
league
subsidized
they are run
championship
free kick
off side
a throw in
to puzzle
to beat
to argue

Description of the scene:

Suggested roleplays
- In pairs, act out a conversation between the referee and a player who has been shown the red card.
- In pairs, act out a conversation between the referee who has not seen what has happened and one of the linesmen.
- In pairs, act out a conversation about the referee between two fans of the losing team.

Make comments on the following statements:
- There's a lot of violence on football fields.
- The decisions of the referee are always respected by the public.
- Good footballers are terribly expensive.
- People support the cold weather and the rain in a football field.
- A collective hysteria breaks out when a team wins the league
- Football puzzles experts.

Questions on the scene
- What's the referee doing?
- Why is he showing a red card?
- Describe the expression of the man on the floor.
- What's the referee wearing?
- Is he wearing all black?
- And the two players, what are they wearing?
- What's the player standing saying?

True or false. Give reasons
- Football in the USA is very popular.
- Referees are always right.
- A match can be repeated if the referee makes a mistake.
- There is a lot of violence at the stadiums.
- Women football leagues are very popular.
- First division footballers get a lot of money.

Questions based on language functions
- What does the referee say to a linesman if he hasn't seen what happened between two players in a corner of the field?
- What does the linesman say if he hasn't seen anything?
- What does a player say to the referee if he wants to protest because another player has kicked him on the leg?
- How do you think the referee tells a player that he has to be sent off the field/pitch?

Football is a social event that puzzles experts. It's the sport that moves the greatest amount of people everywhere in the world. What's its attraction? What has a game that consists of kicking a ball to try to put it in the other team's goal?

Why are people prepared to pay large sums of money and stand in cold weather and rain in order to see their teams beating up the opponents?

It could be argued that poeple go to enjoy a good match, but that is not so. People go to see their team win. They would rather watch a boring match as long as their team brings the three points home.

And when a team wins the cup collective hysteria breaks out all over the town of the winning team.

Questions

1. What does football do to experts?
2. What does the game consist of?
3. Do people pay money to see the game?
4. Do people make sacrifices to see the games?
5. Do people go to see a good match?
6. What would they rather do?
7. What are football fans really interested in?
8. What happens when a team wins the cup?
9. Can players touch the ball with their hands?
10. Who is the man in black?

Football

1. Have you ever seen a football match?
2. What's your opinion of football?
3. Do many people go to see football in your country?
4. Mention some of the most famous football teams in your country.
5. Have any of them won an international competition?
6. Do you think football players earn a lot of money?
7. Can you mention figures?
8. What do you think of them?
9. Do the referees get something similar? How much do they get per match?
10. Do referees make many mistakes?
11. What sort of mistakes do they make?
12. Can the mistakes of the referees affect the results?
13. What can be done to prevent referees' mistakes?
14. Is the game of football violent?
15. What about football fans? Are they violent?
16. Can you mention any violence you have seen on TV on football fields?
17. Should alcoholic drinks be allowed inside the ground?
18. Are fans violent outside the ground?
19. What should the authorities do about it?
20. Is it safe to go to see a football match?
21. Is attendance rising or falling at football matches?
22. Do you have a stadium in your home town?
23. How many people can sit in it?
24. Is your home team in the first division?
25. Do you have any women football teams?
26. Is there a women's football league in your country?
27. Is it a dangerous game for women?
28. Do you think football clubs should be subsidized?
29. Should they be run like an ordinary firm?
30. What's the difference between European and American football?
31. What do South Americans play, European or American football?
32. What country is the present world champion?
33. Did you see any games of the last World Cup?
34. What's a free kick?
35. When does the referee punish a team with a penalty?
36. What's a foul?
37. What's an off side?
38. What's a throw in? What's a corner?
39. When does a referee show the yellow card?
40. When does a referee show the red card?

46 · Policemen

Glossary
police station
plain clothes
to undergo
rewarding
guns
to catch
to fancy
to pursue
wailing
peril
far from
to beat the streets

Description of the scene:

Suggested roleplays

· In pairs, act out a conversation between the policeman and one of the hooligans.
· In pairs, act out a conversation between the two hooligans after the detective's gone.
· In pairs, act out a conversation between two policemen about this band of hooligans.

Make comments on the following statements:

· Policemen are badly paid for the work they do.
· Policemen are very tall.
· Being a policeman is dangerous.

· Solving crimes is difficult.
· In some countries policemen don't carry guns.
· Directing traffic is part of a policeman's job.
· Being a police woman.

Questions on the scene

· What's the little man showing the two thugs?
· Is the detective very big?
· Are the two thugs big?
· What's on the floor?
· Where are the two men sitting?
· What are they wearing?
· What's the detective wearing?
· What are the houses like?

True or false. Give reasons

· Policemen are catching criminals all day.
· They often save girls from dangerous situations.
· A policeman has no regular meal times.
· Divorce is high among policemen.
· Policemen often fire their guns in the street.
· The main job of a policeman is to direct the traffic.

Questions based on language functions

· What does a policeman say if he wants to ask a a suspect to show him his papers?
· What does the man say to refuse to show the policeman his identity papers?
· How does a policeman in a car say to a motorist to pull up at one side of the road?
· How does a policeman invite a police woman to have something to drink during their patrol?

Would you like to be a policeman?

Most young children would. It must be very exciting for a young mind to fancy himself catching criminals all the time. Pursuing robbers in fast wailing cars, or saving beautiful girls from imminent peril.

However, the truth is far from being so attractive. According to a retired police officer, eighty percent of their time is spent either on the beat around the streets. Or watching and following suspects. They have no regular meal times or working hours. Their family life suffers badly from the long hours spent away from home and divorce cases are high among policemen.

Questions

1. What would many children like to be?
2. What is exciting for a young mind?
3. How do policemen pursue robbers?
4. How do they think they can help young girls?
5. Is the truth as attractive as that?
6. What do policemen do most of the time?
7. When do they have their meals?
8. Does family life suffer?
9. Why?
10. Is divorce frequent among policemen?

Policemen

1. Have you ever been to a police station?
2. What different types of policemen do you have in your country?
3. Do you have plain-clothes policemen?
4. Who investigates the crimes?
5. Do you have police cars?
6. What sort of crimes do the police investigate? Mention some.
7. Which police direct the traffic?
8. Is it difficult to be a policeman in your country?
9. What sort of training do they have to undergo?
10. Do they have to be tall?
11. How tall do they have to be?
12. Do they have to know any particular language or have special knowledge?
13. What qualifications do they have to have to be accepted?
14. Do you think being a policeman is a rewarding job?
15. Do people like policemen in your country?
16. Is it a dangerous job?
17. Mention some dangerous situations a policeman has to face.
18. Are policemen well paid for the work they do?
19. What do policemen do at football matches?
20. Would you like to be a policeman?
21. What job would you like to do?
22. What's the most exciting part of a policeman's job?
23. Would you like directing traffic? Why not?
24. Would you like solving crimes?
25. What steps would you take to solve one?
26. Do you think it's difficult to find criminals?
27. Would you like questioning suspects?
28. What methods would you use?
29. How can you tell if they are telling the truth?
30. Do you think the police torture people suspected of a crime?
31. Do you think policemen have to do a lot of paper work?
32. Mention some paper work a policeman may have to do.
33. In Great Britain policemen don't carry guns. What do you think of that?
34. Should policemen fire their guns in the street?
35. What do you think of car pursuits?
36. Is it worth risking people's lives in order to catch a criminal?
37. What hours does a policeman work?
38. How old should policemen be?
39. Once they get older, what sort of work should they do?
40. At what age should a policeman retire from the beat?

47 · A street market

Glossary

bargains
auction
goods
receipt
antiques
stall
stall-holders
gimmicks
to get by
to get warm
stolen
wide-eyed
pedlar
coppers
brass
heater
cutlery

Description of the scene:

Suggested roleplays

- In pairs, act out a conversation between a customer and a street market dealer.
- In pairs, act out a conversation between two women shopping in a street market.
- In pairs, act out a converstation between a stallholder offering three towels for the price of one.

Make comments on the following statements

- A street market is fascinating.
- There are incredible offers.
- Gold watches are very cheap.
- You can buy a masterpiece on an antique stall.
- Silver cutlery may have belonged to royalty.
- Stall holders have to get up very early.

Questions on the scene

- Who's the customer, the man with the glasses or the man watching?
- What's the man examining?
- How many different things can you see on the stall?
- What are they wearing?
- What about the other stall, what do they sell?
- Can you describe the customers?
- What's hanging over their heads?

True or false. Give reasons

- In a street market things are cheaper than in a shop.
- Supermarkets are similar to street markets.
- Stallholders offer two or three things for the price of one.
- The life of these people in winter is hard.
- Stolen good are often sold in street markets.
- Prices are fixed and you can't bargain in street markets.

Questions based on language functions

- What does the customer say to the seller if he wants to examine the goods?
- What does the seller say to refuse letting him examine the things for sale?
- What does the client say to the antique dealer to make him lower the price?
- What does the dealer say to refuse to lower the price of the old 'masterpiece'?
- How does the policeman say to the Stallholder that he can't sell things in the street without permission?

I'm always fascinated in a street market. As a child I used to go to my local street market which was held every Saturday in the main square. There, I watched wide-eyed the incredible offers of the stallholder soffering not two, but three blankets for the price of one. Dark-faced Moroccans trying to sell their merchandise: gold bracelets or watches that looked incredibly beautiful and amazingly cheap. Old fat women who sold used clothes for a few coppers. Then, there were the antique dealers that were the most fascinating of all. Clocks and furniture that had belonged to royalty and nobility; old copper pots and pans, brass bed heaters and silver cutlery that people had used hundreds of years ago.

Questions

1. What fascinates the writer?
2. Where did he use to go as a child?
3. What day of the week did the market take place?
4. How many blankets did the stall holder offer for sale?
5. What did Moroccans offer for sale?
6. What did the old fat women sell?
7. What was the most fascinating of all?
8. Who had the furniture belonged to?
9. What were the pots and pans made of?
10. Was the cutlery very old?

A street market

1. Have you ever bought anything at a street market?
2. Are there many in your country?
3. What are they like?
4. Can you get bargains?
5. What day of the week do they take place?
6. Can you buy quality goods in street markets?
7. Mention some of the things you can buy in them.
8. What are the advantages of buying in a street market?
9. What are the disadvantages?
10. Have you been to an auction in a street market?
11. Are the goods they sell specially prepared for this sale?
12. If the things you buy are no good, can you return them?
13. Do you get a receipt when you buy something?
14. Is there a famous street market in your country?
15. Are prices fixed or you can bargain?
16. Can you get any antiques in these markets?
17. Do stall-holders talk much?
18. Do you remember what they say?
19. Are there any gimmicks to attract people? what?
20. Can you pay with a credit card at these stalls?
21. Will they accept cheques?
22. Would you like to work on one of these stalls?
23. What would you say to possible clients?
24. What would you like to sell?
25. Do you think they earn good money, or just enough to get by?
26. At what time does a street market start business?
27. At what time do you think they have to get up?
28. How many hours do they work?
29. At what time do they 'close'?
30. Is it tiring work?
31. Is it hard working on a stall in winter?
32. How do you get warm?
33. Is it good or bad for the health working on a stall?
34. If they only work on Saturdays, what do you think they do the other days?
35. Are there street markets on weekdays?
36. Are these markets unfair competition for shops?
37. Are you in favour or against street markets in general?
38. Could stolen goods be sold in a street market?
39. Would you buy something extremely cheap suspecting it is stolen?
40. Do you think street markets have a future?

48 · Writing

Glossary
pen-friends
alive
news reader
to prevent
scripts
to research
to flow out

Description of the scene:

Suggested roleplays
- In pairs, act out a conversation between the editor and the writer.
- In pairs, act out a conversation between two writers talking about the book they are writing.
- In pairs, act out a conversation between two journalists covering the trip of the King of Nepal.

Make comments on the following statements:
- Reading is better than watching TV.
- Young people don't read very much.
- Writers get a lot of money.
- Writers work many hours a day.
- Many journalists finish up by writing books.
- It may take years to write a book.
- Writing short stories is very difficult.

Questions on the scene
- Describe the expression of the writer.
- Does he feel inspired today?
- What's on the floor?
- Is he using a computer?
- What's he wearing?
- Would you say that he is a modern or an old fashion writer?
- What would you say about the furniture of the place?

True or false. Give reasons
- Writing is hard work.
- A good historical book may take years to write.
- Good writers are rich.
- Children don't like reading.
- Writers do a lot of research in libraries.
- Sometimes writers spend hours without writing a single line.
- A writer is the same as a journalist.

Questions based on language functions
- What does the editor say to ask the writer if he has finished the book?
- What does the writer say to inform the editor that he hasn't written half the book yet?
- What does the editor say to ask the writer to hurry with his book?
- How does the editor ask the writer to be present in the presentation of his book?
- How does the writer refuse to go to the presentation?

Would you like to be a writer? Many people would answer «yes» to that question. The opinion we all have about writers is that they get a lot of money just by writing a few lines about something or other. However, the truth is that the life of a writer can be very hard. Writers work from six to eight hours a day and spend a long time reading and researching in libraries for the subject they are writing about.

Besides, writing is hard work. It is not easy to put your thoughts down on paper. Sometimes a writer may spend an hour looking at the screen of his computer or his typewriter, without writing a single line. then, suddenly the inspiration comes and the words flow out.

Writing is an art. The reader must be able to see the scene being described through the writer's words. The reader must feel the sentiments of the characters of the book through the lines s/he's reading.

Questions

1. Would many people like to be writers?
2. What's the opinion of people about writers?
3. Is the life of a writer hard?
4. How many hours a day do writers work?
5. What do they do besides writing?
6. Is it easy to put your thoughts down on paper?
7. Has a writer inspiration all the time?
8. What happens when the writer is inspired?
9. What must the reader see in his/her mind?
10. What must the reader feel in his/her mind?

Writing

1. Do you like writing?
2. What sort of things do you like writing?
3. Do you write many letters?
4. Do you have pen-friends in other countries?
5. Have you ever written for the school newspaper?
6. Have you ever written a story?
7. What was it about?
8. How long was it?
9. Did you get any money for it?
10. Did you have it published?
11. Is writing hard?
12. Would you like to be a writer?
13. Do writers get a lot of money in your country?
14. How many hours a day do writers work?
14. Can you mention any good writers who are alive?
15. Do you remember any good writers of past days?
16. Have you read any old books?
17. Is the style the same as today's?
18. What's the difference?
19. Which way of writing do you prefer, modern or old?
20. Is it easy to write a book?
21. How long does it take to write a book?
22. Does a book have to be planned, or written as it goes along?
23. What sort of stories do you like reading?
24. Have you read any best sellers lately?
25. Do computers help writers? in what way?
26. Have you ever written anything directly into a computer?
27. What are the advantages and disadvantages?
28. Which other people earn their living writing?
29. Would you like to be a journalist?
30. What sort of things do journalists write?
31. What's the difference between a journalist and a writer?
32. What different kinds of journalists are there? sports, political, etc?
33. Can TV news readers be considered journalists?
34. Do many people read books in your country?
35. Should people read more?
36. Did people read more in the old days?
37. Does TV help or prevent reading?
38. Would you like to write for TV?
39. Would you like to write a play?
40. What's the difference between writing books, plays or TV scripts?

49 · Painting

Glossary
to reach
portrait
to invest
landscapes
still life
watercolour
brush
bid
gift
to spread
canvas
to splash

· What is he wearing?
· Can you see any other pictures in the room?

True or false. Give reasons

· The Mona Lisa was painted by Leonardo Da Vinci.
· Michelangelo painted the Sistine Chapel.
· A picture can be painted without a brush.
· An artist is born with that gift.
· Often an artist reaches immortality after s/he has died.
· Modern pictures are difficult to understand.
· Picasso was an old Italian painter.
· Salvador Dalí was French.

Description of the scene:

Suggested roleplays

· In pairs, act out a conversation between an artist and a customer.
· In pairs, act out a conversation between two people looking at a modern picture.
· In pairs, act out a conversation between two modern painters talking about their abstract pictures.
· In a group, act out a conversation in an auction. An old master is being sold for a fortune.

Make comments on the following statements:

· Modern pictures are difficult to understand.
· Money invested on pictures is good a good investment.
· Picasso's cubic painting is baffling.
· Montmartre is famous for its painters
· Salvador Dalí was a very peculiar man.
· The Sistine Chapel is the greatest work of Michelangelo.

Questions on the scene

· What's the man doing?
· What has he got in his right hand?
· And what has he got in his left hand?
· What is he painting?
· What fruit is he painting?
· Can you describe the face of the painter?

Questions based on language functions

· What does a man say to a modern painter if he wants to know which way to hang a picture?
· How does the painter say that the legs are the top part of the picture?
· What does a man say to a painter if he wants to know the price of a picture?
· What does the painter say to a person if he wants to tell him that his pictures are not for sale?
· How do you think the owner of a mansion tells a painter that nobody is allowed to paint inside his property?

There are many millions of artists painting pictures all over the world. However, very few of them earn their living painting. Most of them spend their lives spreading paints on canvas that they will never sell. Others reach immortality after they are dead and their pictures are sold at auctions for the benefit of the fortunate buyers that bought them for a handful of pounds or dollars. I must confess that art puzzles me. I don't know what the experts base their ideas of beauty on. I can understand about the old masters and the different tones on the canvas, but, can anyone tell me what to look for in one of Picasso's cubic paintings? Or which way to place the picture when I'm looking at some modern thing, that for all I know is a lot of paint splashed on the canvas by a five-year-old child?

Questions

1. Are there many artists?
2. Do many of them earn their living painting?
3. What do most of them do?
4. When do some artists reach immortality?
5. Who gets the benefit of the selling of the pictures?
6. What does the writer confess?
7. What doesn't he know?
8. What can the writer understand?
9. What does he say about Picasso's paintings?
10. What does a modern picture look like?

Painting

1. Have you ever painted a picture?
2. What do you think of it? Is it difficult or easy?
3. Would you like to earn your living painting?
4. Do you know anybody who does?
5. Have you been to a private exhibition of pictures?
6. What prices did the pictures reach?
7. What is a portrait?
8. Would you invest money in pictures?
9. Do you have any good painters in your country?
10. Can you remember the names of the 'old masters'?
11. Which country was famous for its painters?
12. Who painted the famous 'Sistine Chapel'?
13. Who painted the Mona Lisa?
14. Which do you like best, landscapes, portraits, still life?
15. What's the difference?
16. What does 'painting in oils' mean?
17. What is 'watercolour painting'?
18. Can you explain what 'cubism' is?
19. Mention the artist who started it.
20. What is 'modern painting'?
21. Do you understand it?
22. In what style would you categorize Picasso?
24. What do you think of Salvador Dalí?
25. Are there any Museums or Picture Galleries in your country?
26. What are the names of the galleries?
27. Which famous painters can you find in them?
28. Can anyone paint without a brush?
29. Do you know the name of the painter whose pictures have cost most?
30. What's the picture that reached the highest bid in an auction?
31. Do you know how much it was?
32. Do painters see their work appreciated during their lives?
33. Does an artist learn to paint or is he/she born with the gift?
34. How long do you think it takes to learn to paint?
35. Paris has a district called 'Montmartre'. What is it famous for?
36. Do you have anything like that in your country?
37. What sort of life does an artist lead?
38. Have you seen artists painting on street pavements? What do you think of them?
39. Some modern painters use sprays to paint huge walls. What do you think of that?
40. What other way of painting can you think of? Have you ever painted your kitchen?

50 · Sailing

Glossary

to sail
liner
dead calm
fridges
canned
safe
gale
graceful
spread wide
weather-beaten
worst of all
to flop down
scurvy

· What are these two men on the right doing?
· What's the weather like?
· What are they wearing?

True or false. Give reasons

· Columbus discovered America because he knew it was there.
· The Indians were expecting them and became good friends.
· Magellan was the first man to go round the world.
· Saling ships can advance without wind.
· A sailing ship can advance even if the wind is blowing against it.
· Juan Sebastian Elcano went with Cristopher Columbus.
· Magellan didn't carry a radio transmitter in his ship.

Questions based on language functions

· What does the captain say to the sailors in a sailing ship when he wants to start off?
· What does the captain say to the sailors when he wants the ship to stop?
· What does the captain say to the sailors if he wants to go faster?
-- How do you think the captain will tell the crew to drop anchor?

Description of the scene:

Suggested roleplays

· In pairs, act out a conversation between the captain and one of the sailors.
· In pairs, act out a conversation between two sailors in the Santa María on the 12th October 1492.
· In a group, act out a conversation between the sailors of the ship of Magellan when they discovered the straight that led to the Pacific Ocean.

Make comments on the following statements:

· Going on a sailing ship is very exciting.
· Sailing around the world makes you feel free.
· A solitary sailor went round the world in a little sailing ship a few years ago.
· Seamen were very brave in the old days sailing across unknown seas.
· Many seamen died of scurvy in the old days. This was due to the lack of vegetables in their diet.

Questions on the scene

· How many people are sailing the ship?
· What kind of ship is it?
· Do you think it's windy?
· Are they far away from land?

Sailing with the wind! When I see those graceful little boats with their white sails spread wide, skimming over the waves, I can't help wondering how they do it. It has always been a mystery to me how a sailing boat can go against the wind. It is easy enough to make something run with the wind I'm sure that even I could do that, but another thing is to make something advance against the wind. I was told by a weather-beaten seaman that they don't advance straight into the wind, but they take it diagonally and advance in zigzag, but even so, it seems to me incredibly difficult. Worst of all, they say, it's the total absence of wind. When the sails flop down dead, the ship stops. That dead calm can go on for days and even weeks.

Questions

1. Is the writer a good seaman?
2. What does he wonder?
3. Is it difficult to run with the wind?
4. Is it easy to advance against the wind?
5. Does a sailing ship advance straight into the wind?
6. What is the worst thing that may happen to a sailing ship?
7. Who said that to the writer?
8. What happens when the sails flop down dead?
9. Can that state of things go on for a long time?
10. Have you ever sailed?

Sailing

1. Have you ever sailed?
2. Do you like it?
3. Is it dangerous?
4. Do you think seamen should learn how to swim?
5. Would you like to sail in a big sailing ship?
6. Do you have one in your country?
7. How many seamen are necessary to man one of those big ships?
8. How do they pull the sails down?
9. How many sails do they have?
10. Do you know their names?
11. What's the difference between a sailing ship and a liner?
12. Which one is more exciting?
13. In which epoch did sails begin to be used by man?
14. What did they use before then?
15. How do sailing ships advance against the wind?
16. What do sailing ships do when there is no wind?
17. Do you think the 'dead calm' can last very long?
18. What would you do if you were the captain of a sailing ship and were caught by 'dead calm' in the middle of the ocean?
19. Do you think that life at sea in those days was hard?
20. What sort of work would the seamen do?
21. How did they sleep?
22. Did the men have private toilets?
23. Had those ships fridges?
24. What sort of food did they eat?
25. Did they have fresh meat or eggs?
26. What about vegetables? Had they frozen or canned vegetables in those days?
27. What about the water? Where did they keep the fresh water?
28. What would happen to the water after two or three months at sea?
29. What do you think about the health of those people?
30. Do you think the captain and officers would share the same food and water?
31. What would you do if you were the captain?
32. Was it safe to sail on those ships across the ocean 500 years ago?
33. What do you think of Christopher Columbus crossing an unknown sea?
34. What would you do if you were caught by a storm in a saling ship?
35. Would you pull the sails down or leave them up?
36. Would you sail with the gale force wind or against it?
37. Do you remember the name of the first man to go round the world in a sailing ship?
38. What was the nationallity of Juan Sebastian Elcano?
39. Who was Magellan?
40. What do you think of their adventure? How long did they take to finish the trip?

FONDO EDITORIAL STANLEY

ENGLISH

3000 TESTS ELEMENTARY LEVEL
KEYS 3000 TESTS
2000 TESTS ADVANCED LEVEL
KEYS 2000 TESTS
1500 STRUCTURED TESTS I
1500 STRUCTURED TESTS II
1500 STRUCTURED TESTS III
KEYS STRUCTURED TESTS
DIDACTIC CROSSWORDS I
BILINGUAL BUSINESS LETTERS
NEW GUIDE TO BUSINESS LETTERS
ENGLISH GRAMMAR I (N/E)
ENGLISH GRAMMAR II (N/E)
ENGLISH GRAMMAR III (N/E)
KEYS ENGLISH GRAMMAR
2000 BILINGUAL PHRASES I
2000 BILINGUAL PHRASES II
2000 BILINGUAL PHRASES III
GUIDE OF PREPOSITIONS
USING PREPOSITIONS - EXERCISES
159 TRANSLATIONS I
159 TRANSLATIONS II
159 TRANSLATIONS III
159 TRANSLATIONS IV
FILL IN THE GAPS I
FILL IN THE GAPS II
FILL IN THE GAPS III
KEYS FILL IN THE GAPS
DICTATIONS IN ENGLISH I
DICTATIONS IN ENGLISH II
GUIDE TO PHRASAL VERBS
USING PHRASAL VERBS
ENGLISH VERBS ONE BY ONE
MY ENGLISH TELLTALE
CONVERSATION IN ACTION - Let´s talk!
THE IRREGULAR VERBS AND MODALS
1000 EVERYDAY IDIOMS IN BUSINESS
A TO ZED, A TO ZEE · A GUIDE TO THE DIFFERENCES BETWEEN BRITISH AND AMERICAN ENGLISH
EL INGLÉS PROHIBIDO
FALSE FRIENDS · FALSOS AMIGOS

FRANÇAIS

1000 TESTS EN FRANÇAIS I
1000 TESTS EN FRANÇAIS II
1000 TESTS EN FRANÇAIS III
1000 TESTS EN FRANÇAIS IV
1000 TESTS EN FRANÇAIS V
5000 CLÉS
DICTÉS EN FRANÇAIS I-A
DICTÉS EN FRANÇAIS I-B
DICTÉS EN FRANÇAIS I-C
MOTS CROISÉS DIDACTIQUES
L'ILE MYSTÉRIEUSE -Lecture
20.000 LIEUES SOUS LES MERS -Lecture
LES TROIS MOUSQUETAIRES - Lecture
LE COMPTE DE MONTE CRISTO -Lecture
UN CAPITAINE DE QUINZE ANS -Lecture
MICHEL STROGOFF -Lecture
QUI SAIT? -Lecture
LA FAMILLE LENOIR -Lecture
TRADUIRE AUJOURD'HUI 1
TRADUIRE AUJOURD'HUI 2
MON BILAN GRAMMATICAL
NOUVEAU GUIDE DE CORRESPONDANCE COMMERCIALE

GUÍAS PARA VIAJAR

GUÍA DEL VIAJERO - INGLÉS
CONVERSATION GUIDE - SPANISH
GUÍA DEL VIAJERO - ALEMÁN
SPRACHFURER KONVERSATION -SPANISCH
GUÍA DEL VIAJERO - FRANCÉS
GUIDE CONVERSATION - ESPAGNOL
GUÍA DEL VIAJERO ITALIANO
GUIDA DI CONVERSAZIONE - ESPAGNOLO
GUÍA DEL VIAJERO - PORTUGUÉS

ESPAÑOL

TESTS ESPAÑOL I
TESTS ESPAÑOL II
TESTS ESPAÑOL III
TESTS ESPAÑOL IV
TESTS ESPAÑOL V
CLAVES TESTS ESPAÑOL
DICTADOS EN ESPAÑOL I-A
DICTADOS EN ESPAÑOL I-B
DICTADOS EN ESPAÑOL I-C
CRUCIGRAMAS DIDÁCTICOS I
CRUCIGRAMAS DIDÁCTICOS II
CRUCIGRAMAS DIDÁCTICOS III
GRAMÁTICA ESPAÑOLA
CLAVES GRAMÁTICA ESPAÑOLA

Lecturas graduadas en español:
· LA FAMILIA PEREZ
· ¿QUIÉN SABE?
· LA ISLA MISTERIOSA
· 20.000 LEGUAS DE VIAJE SUBMARINO
· EL CONDE DE MONTECRISTO
· LOS TRES MOSQUETEROS
· UN CAPITÁN DE 15 AÑOS
· MIGUEL STROGOFF